Leatherhead Food International

CUSTOMER SATISFACTION

Dotun Adebanjo

Published by
Leatherhead Publishing
a division of
Leatherhead International Limited
Randalls Road, Leatherhead, Surrey KT22 7RY, UK

First Edition 2002
ISBN No: 1 904007 44 9

Printed and bound in the UK by IBT Global, 1B Barking Business Centre, 25 Thames Road, Barking, London IG11 OJP

CONTENTS

PREFACE

The satisfaction of customers continues to be an important cornerstone for successful businesses worldwide. In a more competitive world, suppliers continue to seek ways to satisfy ever-increasing customer demands and expectations. For many years, Leatherhead Food International has been at the forefront of helping food companies worldwide to improve a range of their business and operational practices. The idea of this guidebook was developed following a study of UK food industries, which indicated that there was a need for an articulation of a best practice perspective and tools to assist companies in the sector to improve their focus on customers.

This book is primarily directed at executives with responsibility for developing policies and making decisions that affect customers. The contents are also targeted at companies that supply other companies (business-to-business) rather than companies that supply the general public (business-to-consumer).

The material in this book is intended to give an overview of the concepts that underpin the field of customer satisfaction, while at the same time illustrating some of the concepts with case studies and a toolkit that provides practical assistance for organisations. The book is intended to be concise, interesting and informative to organisations across all sectors, although most of the case studies are from the food industry.

For practical reasons, the material in this book has been split into three distinct parts as follows:

✦ Part 1 presents an informative overview of the concepts of customer satisfaction and discusses topics such as customer care, understanding customer needs, customer value, branding, loyalty and customer relationship management.

✦ Part 2 presents a number of case studies from different industries, with the food industry being predominant. These are intended to provide a view of how different organisations have successfully approached improvements to different aspects of customer satisfaction.

✦ Part 3 presents a toolkit that would be helpful in assisting companies improve their focus on customers. Companies with limited customer service resources would find the toolkit particularly useful. The toolkit is designed to be non-prescriptive and flexible in nature.

Financial assistance for this project was provided by DEFRA.

It is hoped that readers of this book will find the material useful in their aim to improve the levels of service and satisfaction given to their customers.

Dotun Adebanjo
University of Liverpool

PART 1: THE PRINCIPLES OF CUSTOMER SATISFACTION

1. INTRODUCTION

Increasing customer sophistication, globalisation, greater choice and technology have brought about a quiet revolution in the dynamics of supplier-customer relationships. These and other factors have affected the sometimes complex inter-relationships between product and service delivery across all business sectors. Consequently, the focus of customer satisfaction has widened from the traditional retailer-consumer dimension to include other stakeholders such as manufacturers, sub-manufacturers, third-party service providers and even internal customers.

What is perhaps truer than ever before is that companies that wish to remain in business and be successful must not only seek to win and satisfy customers but also strive to keep them. For numerous reasons, many of which will be described in this book, it is no longer enough to compete on just price and product quality. In many cases, there will probably be a cheaper competitor while many customers take a certain level of product quality as a given. The result is that many organisations continue to seek ways of understanding and satisfying their customers.

The need to understand customers and their needs and to keep them satisfied and loyal has led to a rash of customer-related terminology and concepts such as customer care, customer relationship management (CRM), e-loyalty, customer focus, customer delight, customer value and customer cost, to mention a few. While many organisations have made and continue to make significant progress with respect to meeting and, sometimes, exceeding customer requirements, others continue to struggle to keep their customers or attract new ones. Confusion about the various customer concepts has not served many of these companies positively in their quest to retain and, where possible, increase market share and hence profitability.

Irrespective of the route they have taken in their drive to satisfy customers, successful companies have found that they need to become more customer-centric. The limitations of traditional systems, whereby organisational structures and processes were designed to meet the needs of the organisation rather than those of the customer, are now increasingly being recognised and accepted. Customer-successful organisations are flexible in their approaches to dealing with customers and their requirements.

In terms of the customer experience, it is also being recognised that focusing effort exclusively on direct customer-facing activities and service attributes such as on-time and in-full performance indicators is no longer sufficient to give organisations competitive advantage. Satisfying customers has increasingly become a combination of wider factors, such as communication, sales and after-sales support, price, convenience of transacting business, and product attributes.

1.1   The Food Industry Perspective

Within the UK food industry, a lot of effort has been directed at meeting the needs of the consumer. This is evident in the adoption of initiatives such as Efficient Consumer Response (ECR). Once again, greater consumer choice and awareness have meant that retailers have become more competitive and more sensitive to consumer behaviour and market trends. In addition, the trend towards convenience shopping has meant that big retailers have become very powerful in the food and drinks sector. In their effort to satisfy the end consumer, the retailers have become more demanding of their suppliers/manufacturers, who now need to be more flexible in their operations.

The on-going challenge for the food industry is to engineer a complete turnaround in the traditionally adversarial relationships between retailers and manufacturers. It is important to suppliers, customers and the end consumer that suppliers and customers work increasingly as partners in order to develop win-win strategies. While this need has been recognised and some progress has been made, the emphasis and success achieved in customer satisfaction between manufacturers and retailers do not compare with those between retailers and consumers. The situation becomes more complex when ingredients and raw materials manufacturers are also considered as suppliers to the 'final product' manufacturers. While larger companies in the food supply chain typically have some resources to dedicate to customer satisfaction, it is the smaller companies that face the greatest challenges in achieving, understanding and adopting comprehensive customer satisfaction and retention strategies.

This book examines the issues involved with customer satisfaction and will enable greater awareness and understanding of practices and ideas that would improve levers of customer satisfaction within the food industry. In particular, the book focuses primarily on customer satisfaction in the upper part of the food supply chain (manufacturer-manufacturer and manufacturer-retailer) as opposed to the satisfaction between retailers and consumers, which has been the subject of many initiatives. In addition, the book presents selected case studies from within and outside the food industry in an effort to show what successful companies are achieving with respect to satisfying their customers. It is expected that suggestions made in this book will create opportunities for companies to improve their current levels of customer satisfaction.

1.2 The Growth of Customer Development

The importance of customers to businesses has long been recognised. The increasing demands of customers have meant that the view of how organisations relate and provide service to customers has evolved significantly over the years. Fig 1.1. presents a view of this evolution.

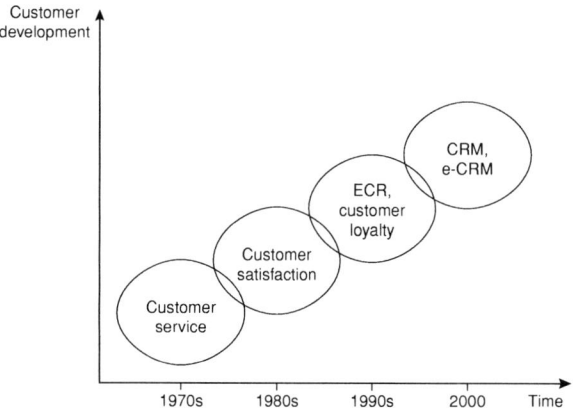

Fig. 1.1. The evolution of customer development

2. UNDERSTANDING CUSTOMER REQUIREMENTS

2.1   Defining Customers

In order to be focused on customers and to meet their needs, it is important to know exactly what a customer is. In particular, it is important to make a distinction between 'customers' and 'buyers'. A customer has developed a 'custom' of buying your products or buying from your company. To have a 'true' customer presumes a history of continuous interaction and frequent purchase. An organisation that purchases from time to time only and that purchases competing products on a regular basis is probably more of a 'buyer' that a 'customer'.

In more economic terms, a customer is an organisation to which you provide goods and services in return for payment. Such payment may be monetary or may be goods and services. To enable continuation of business interaction, both parties should gain benefits from their association.

Most organisations are likely to have not only different customers but also different classes of customer. A food manufacturing company, for example, may class retailers, wholesalers, distributors and end consumers as different classes of customer. Similarly, a third-party logistics company will classify both the manufacturer (or seller) and the retailer (or buyer) as customers. It is important to note that different classes of customer have different needs that should be understood and fulfilled.

2.1.1   Customer vs consumer

It is important for an organisation to distinguish between the customer and the consumer. The customer would typically be another organisation that makes use of or sells the products made, while the consumer would be the end user of the product. It should be understood that these two groups have different

6

requirements that need to be reflected in the attributes of the products and services supplied by the organisation. For example, a customer may place considerable emphasis on accurate invoicing and on-time delivery while a consumer may be more interested in product packaging and quality.

2.2   Why Understand Customer Requirements?

Satisfying customers is about doing what matters best. It is generally accepted that the customer should identify the factors that matter most. This gives the supplier a fairly accurate idea of what the customer wants and fulfilling this is an important step towards achieving satisfaction. Within the food industry, it is estimated that 90% of new products fail. While some of these failures will be attributable to problems such as financial management, inadequate production facilities and supplier problems, a substantial number of product withdrawals are the result of weak or inadequate demand. This is typically a result of not understanding the needs of one type of customer – the end consumer.

Many organisations in the food industry appear to adopt the approach of developing and launching a product first and then trying to 'sell' through aggressive marketing. This is even more likely if the product has been successful in a different market or country. While this approach sometimes works, with impressive results, more often than not organisations struggle to recoup the cost of their development and marketing.

The importance of understanding customer needs affects more than just new products. Concentrating on improving attributes that do not matter greatly to the customer can lead to the delivery or perception of delivery of poor value. Where retailers are the customers, this can lead to operational problems and, consequently, dissatisfaction. In addition, expending resources on low-value-adding attributes also implies that the supplier makes poor use of its resources.

2.2.1   *Implicit and explicit requirements*

Inability to understand the nature of implicit and explicit needs can lead to unexpected concerns for suppliers. Although it is commonly acknowledged that customers should be the ones to specify requirements and, consequently, the determinants of satisfaction, it is important to note that, on their own initiative, customers often only state their explicit requirements. They generally have other needs, which are implicit. Understanding explicit needs has some key implications for suppliers:

- These are likely to be the same requirements that the customer has given to other suppliers, and by fulfilling them the company is probably not doing significantly more than the competition.
- The company is likely to be complacent and to believe that it is satisfying its customers by meeting their explicit needs.
- Customers are more likely to complain if their explicit needs are not met than if their implicit needs are not met.

As an example, retailers are likely to specify product attributes and delivery schedules, which can be seen as explicit requirements. Implicit requirements could include factors such as correct invoicing, timely invoicing, speed of resolution of complaints and ease of placing of orders. Some of these factors may be described as agents of dissatisfaction or hygiene factors, i.e. factors whose presence may not directly lead to satisfaction but whose absence is likely to lead to dissatisfaction. It is important that suppliers put in place systems to satisfy the hygiene factors that customers would take for granted.

In summary, the understanding of customer needs not only plays a vital role in achieving satisfaction but can have an impact on the operational dynamics of the supplier. Furthermore, there is a need to understand the needs of various customers and various types of customer and balance these needs as far as possible.

2.3   The Concept of Customisation

As customers have become more demanding and diverse in their needs, many suppliers/producers have adopted customisation in an effort to maintain customer focus and provide added value. More flexible work processes and better communication methods enable customisation in high volumes and reasonable cost. This is particularly relevant to the food industry, where it is not uncommon for one producer to manufacture different versions of the same product to often slightly different specifications. This is typified in the production of branded products and private-label products for different retailers/wholesalers. Furthermore, it is not uncommon for private-label goods to be specified in economy and premium quality categories.

In order to reduce unnecessary cost and complexity, and still produce customer value, it is important that suppliers understand the different types of customisation possible and the characteristics/limitations of each. The key issues in customisation are:

- Adding value – it is important to understand how the products impact on customers and their businesses.

- Brand differentiation – as more and more products become commoditised, it has become more important to differentiate company brands. The service provided with such products is an important part of brand differentiation. For example, premium clothes manufacturers and restaurants promote the shopping experience and the dining experience as part of their brand differentiation.

- Social pressures to customise – customers and consumers are increasingly seeking exclusivity and this implies that companies must seek ways to match the need for exclusivity with the operational efficiencies of mass production.

Different practitioners have described the different customisation types as shown in Table 2.I. The historical development of customisation is shown in Fig. 2.1.

TABLE 2.I
Different customisation types

Gilmore & Pine (1997)	Sharma (1987)	Lampel & Mintzberg (1996)	Shapiro (1997) Konijnendijk (1993)
	Standard (no options)	Pure standardisation	**Catalogue (Make to stock)**
Cosmetic		Segmented standardisation	
Adaptive	Standard, customer-specified options	Customised standardisation	**Custom-built (Make to order)**
Collaborative	Standard, modified to customer spec.	Tailored standardisation	**Custom-designed (Engineer to order)**
Transparent	Customised product	Pure customisation	

Generally speaking, there are three types of industrial product lines, which are represented in the last column of Table 2.I. Other customisation types mentioned in the table can be seen as subdivisions of these three.

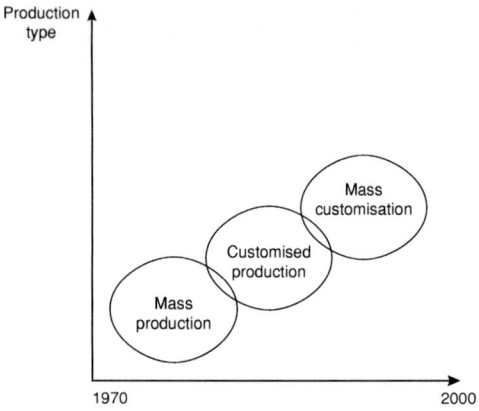

Fig. 2.1. The historical development of customisation

2.3.1 Catalogue products (standard, pure, cosmetic or segmented customisation

These are standard products where no modification is made to the product itself. However, a variation of this is the 'cosmetic' category, whereby the same product is put into different packages for different customers or for marketing (e.g. promotions) or legal (e.g. labelling laws) purposes. For example, Company A may produce only one brand of corn flakes to a fixed recipe and in 500-g packaging. In a cosmetic variation, the company would package the product in 600-g packs (during a 20% extra promotion) or 30-g packs (for consumption in the hotel and services sector).

2.3.2 Custom-built products (customised standardisation or adaptive customisation)

These are products that require some modification to the standard design in order to meet customer specification. In the food industry, this will most likely apply to minor changes in product content specification, as may be specified by different retailers. For example, Company B may produce private-labelled corn flakes for three or four retailers with slight differences in recipes.

2.3.3 *Custom-designed products (collaborative/pure customisation or tailored standardisation)*

These are products that have to be uniquely designed or engineered for a specific customer. The first variation, or 'pure customisation', is when the product is completely different from the standard or custom-built products and is characterised by descriptions such as 'novel or innovative products'. The second variation is when a standard or custom-built product is engineered differently and requires more than minor adjustments to product specification. This may be typified in products with unique shape or unique packaging methods that may require a special production line or a changeover of line equipment. For example, Company C could make innovative 'ready-to-eat' corn flakes packs (with milk) or specially-flavoured corn flakes in collaboration with a major retailer).

* * *

The above-mentioned categories are all applicable to the food industry, and it is important that organisations understand the customer requirements and the limitation of their processes before taking on orders. Where substantial line modification or capital equipment is required, the cost should be balanced against the return from the product by considering factors such as production volume, margins and the possibility of using the modifications for other customers' products. In some cases, the investment required will not be justified.

2.4   Establishing Customer Requirements

The ability to establish a system or process that captures the future requirements of customers is vital to being able to fulfil those requirements. Most organisations have a range of methods that enable them to maintain the relevant communication channels with customers. Broadly speaking, ways of finding out customer requirements can be split into direct and indirect methods.

2.4.1 Direct methods

This involves asking customers directly what their requirements are. This may be achieved through any combination of the following:

- Face-to-face meetings – the frequency and format of such meetings will depend on a range of issues, including the organisations involved, product(s) involved, length of relationship and value of trade.

- Telephone discussions – enables a larger number of customers to be contacted at a reasonable cost. This method, in isolation, may not be suited for all relationships and, in particular, key relationships that may involve considerations such as new service design and new customer orientation.

- Questionnaires – customer service questionnaires provide a convenient way of surveying a large customer database. Large questionnaire surveys have the ability to produce good quantitative but, sometimes, limited qualitative data. It is common for organisations to contract out some or all aspects of their surveys.

- Focus groups – commissioning focus groups enables targeted discussion in order to identify the specific needs of customers. Focus groups have a number of advantages, including the opportunity to get instant feedback and the ability to get input from diverse views at one sitting, e.g. a focus group of consumers may consist of people of different ages or occupations.

- Electronic communication – media such as e-mail and faxes are increasingly being used to communicate with customers. However, these methods are more efficient in understanding short-term customer requirements, e.g. late orders or delivery scheduling, than longer-term requirements, e.g. the adoption of alternative packaging methodologies.

2.4.2 Indirect methods

Indirect methods of understanding customers' requirements are more likely to provide a 'big picture' and a market trends perspective rather than an understanding of the requirements of any one customer. Usually, a third party is involved. The more common indirect methods of understanding customer requirements include:

- Independent market surveys – market surveys carried out by independent agencies can give an insight into current and future trends.

- Press articles – these are likely to approach the issue of trends from a consumer 'interest' or 'protection' point of view.

- Conferences – these provide a unique opportunity to have an insight into what other organisations think of trends in customer requirements and satisfaction. In addition, there is usually an opportunity to network with organisations facing the same issues and, often, customers.

- Consultants – specialist consultants work with a range of organisations and generally have an idea of current thinking and trends in addition to successful practices that have been adopted in other organisations.

* * *

Typically, a combination of direct and indirect methods will be applied when a concerted effort to understand customer requirements is undertaken. It is also important to note that, where a customer chain exists, it may be advantageous to apply these methods to both a direct customer and the end consumer or customer. For example, while a food manufacturing company will consider retailers as the primary customer, a timely appreciation of trends in consumer behaviour (organic foods, ethical concerns, etc.) will enable a pro-active approach to fulfilling these requirements before they become retailer-critical.

2.4.3 Interpreting customer requirements

In many instances, customer requirements are expressed in non-technical language. In order to meet these requirements, it may be necessary to translate or convert them into a more technical form. Care must be taken to ensure that the essence of the requirements is not lost in the translation process. One of the more established and effective tools for facilitating this translation is Quality Function Deployment (QFD). QFD enables the needs of the customer to be reflected in the characteristics and design of the product. QFD involves defining customers' (or consumers') product preferences and needs (through market research, focus groups, etc.) and classifying these needs as *customer requirements*. The relative importance of the requirements to the customer is identified and opinions on competing products sought. This enables better appreciation of key product characteristics that should be designed into new product or improved in existing products. Figure 2.2 presents the basic QFD diagram often referred to as the 'house of quality'. QFD is often carried out by a multi-functional team typically comprising representatives from marketing, manufacturing, product design and sales departments. Details on QFD can be found in many quality management/assurance books.

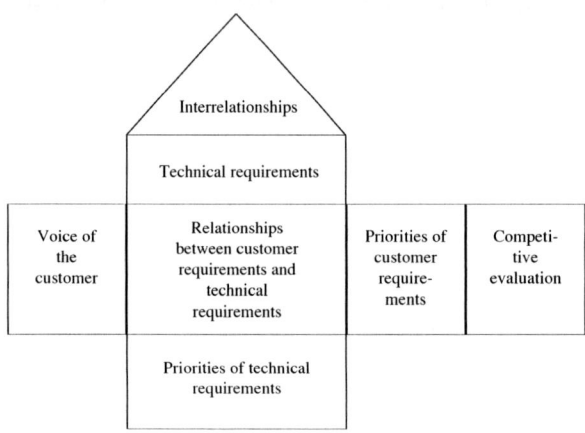

Fig. 2.2. The basic QFD diagram

2.5   Key Summary Points

• Understand the needs of both the customers and the end consumers

• Seek out both implicit and explicit needs

• Appreciate the implications of the different customisation types and determine which is best for your organisation, customers and products

• Establishing customer requirements can be carried out using a range of methods suitable to different companies and their customers

2.6   Further Reading

Cohen L. (1995). *Quality Function Deployment*. Addison Wesley, Massachusetts.

Gilmore J.H., Pine J.B. II. (1997). The four faces of mass customization. *Harvard Business Review*, 75, 1, 91-101.

Hill N. (1999). The seven stages of finding out what matters most to customers. *Measuring Business Excellence*, 3, 1, 31-5.

Konijnendijk P.A. (1993). Dependence and conflict between production and sales. *Industrial Marketing Management*, 22, 161-7.

Lampel J., Mintzberg H. (1996). Customising customisation. *Sloan Management Review*, 21-30.

Smith I. (1997). *Meeting Customer Needs*. Butterworth Heinemann, Oxford.

Spring M., Dalrymple J.F. (2000). Product customisation and manufacturing strategy. *International Journal of Operations and Production Management*, 20, 4, 441-67.

3. CUSTOMER FOCUS AND CARE

3.1   Introduction

The concept of customer focus has gained prominence in recent years. This has been encouraged by the adoption and widespread use of management frameworks such as the EFQM Excellence Model (Fig. 3.1) and The Balanced Scorecard. The EFQM Excellence Model is widely used within Europe as a tool for self-assessment and continuous business improvement. It is also used as the model for the award of prestigious regional, national and international awards. Of the nine criteria that comprise the model, 'customer satisfaction' is the most important and accounts for a weighting of 20% of the model. The fact that an internationally accepted and applied model applies greater weighting to customer satisfaction than business results is a reflection of the appreciation that organisations need to focus primarily on the needs and satisfaction of their customers. The balanced scorecard was developed by Kaplan and Norton with a view to encouraging the use of widespread measures within organisations. Their approach was that, in addition to measuring the financial perspective of their operations, organisations should also measure other perspectives – the customer perspective, the internal business perspective and the innovation and learning perspective. While the customer perspective focuses primarily on the satisfaction of the external customer, the internal business perspective, in part, focuses on the internal processes and practices that would impact on customer satisfaction.

The customer focus concept and these frameworks promote an understanding that the customer is key to the survival of the organisation. While it is understandable that businesses need to make a financial return, this can only be made possible if customer needs and requirements are met or exceeded – hence the focus on customers. Closely associated with the focus on customers is the ability to provide customer care. Customer care is generally viewed as a means for effectively focusing on customers.

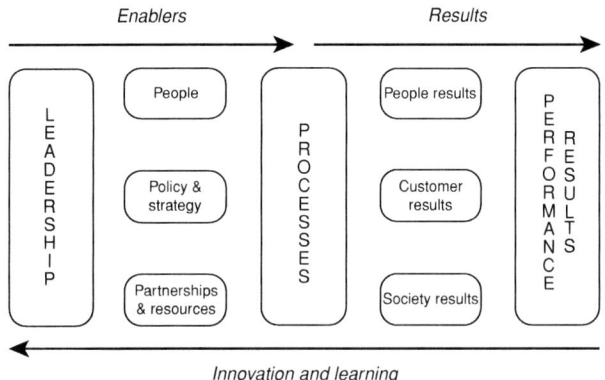

Copyright 1999 EFQM. The model is a registered trademark of the EFQM

Fig. 3.1. The EFQM Excellence Model

3.2   Understanding Customer Focus

Customer focus is commonly identified as a cultural issue. While it encompasses many operational considerations, such as care, service and relationship management, organisations that subscribe to the concept are making a statement of willingness to adopt new practices in their business operations.

The customer must be seen and treated as the centre of the organisation's operations. In a traditionally structured organisation, an effort to focus on customers might result in the following:

- A change of structure – where a functional or hierarchical organisational structure becomes more project/process-based or flatter. It is important to create an organisational structure tailored to improve the ease with which the customer does business with the organisation. This would involve many departments and functions within the organisation. For example, the sales department may be organised so that key customers have designated account managers. The primary aim of any customer-focused organisational structure should be to enable closeness to the customer irrespective of dimensions such as distance, product characteristics, etc. The case study on Magro Brothers (presented in Part 2) shows how they promote closeness to their customers irrespective of considerable geographical distance.

- Modification of processes/procedures – having a focus on the customer would mean that more of an organisation's processes and activities will be customer-facing rather than inward-facing, i.e. they are primarily directed at satisfying the customer. Many organisations have traditionally built business systems around their products or financial systems rather than around customers. Such systems tend to be successful in alienating customers or making them feel unwanted or unappreciated. Improvements would mean that processes across the organisation (ranging from product delivery to invoicing) should be designed to enable better interaction with the customers.

- Redefining of the customer chain – there is a need to identify the internal customer. This will reduce the risk of internal fragmentation negatively affecting the end customer. It is important that all employees understand the impact that their functions have on the customer. This will require the support of senior management in promoting the relevant training and education. Increasingly, organisations are basing performance measurement and reward systems throughout the organisation on customer-focus-related performance.

- Re-examination of customer-related practices – the way in which employees think of, relate to and communicate with the customer will have to be re-examined and, most likely, improved or modified. This approach will rely on the implementation of previous suggestions (e.g. training, company structure and process re-engineering) and the implementation of new practices concerning factors such as communication methods, and complaints handling.

In common with many cultural developments, the concept of customer focus cannot be treated as a project but will need to develop over time. Changing culture tends to be an evolutionary process.

3.2.1 The internal customer

In addition to the organisation having external customers, every employee and every department within that organisation has an internal customer. Typically, the flow of work in most organisations means that responsibility for a product or services passes from one individual (or department) to another individual (or department) until it ultimately ends up with the external customer. Recognising the next individual in the company's process as an internal customer with operational and service requirements will facilitate maximisation of the levels of synergy within the organisation. Ultimately, it will create an environment where everyone has an obligation to focus on his/her customer and this value chain extends beyond the organisation to the external customer. In short, the company is only as strong as its weakest link and this weakness is what is ultimately passed on to the external customer.

When an individual or department recognises who its internal customers are and appreciates that they are all working to meet the needs of the external customer, the tendency is for communication to be improved, conflict reduced, duplication avoided and satisfaction and working relationships optimised. A common way of achieving this is through company-sponsored dialogue – management encouraging departments and individuals to talk to each other in order to determine how to serve each other better.

Robert Johnston has produced a 'how to do it' guide relating to customer-focused systems. His key suggestions are presented as follows:

TABLE 3.1
Customer-focused systems: a quick "how to do it" guide – some suggestions

1. Test out all of your systems and ask: "do they make things easy or difficult for staff and/or customers".
2. Use every means and opportunity to communicate with staff.
3. Develop formal and informal mechanisms for listening to both customers and staff – and do something about what you hear.
4. Have training plans for *everyone* in the organisation.
5. Consider using role models or mentors.
6. Link customer satisfaction to financial and/or non-financial rewards.
7. Calculate the bottom line implications of customer service developments.
8. Consider looking outside the industry for new ideas.
9. Ensure that information from complaints is used to drive improvements throughout the organisation.
10. Involve senior managers directly in the complaints process.
11. Analyse compliments and learn from them too.

Source: Johnston, 2001

3.3 Customer Care

Customer care techniques are most relevant to customer-facing staff. These staff play a vital role in the effective maintenance of business relationships with customers. More often than not, customer-facing staff positions are low in the hierarchy of the organisation (e.g. call centre operators, delivery drivers, office receptionist) but they are usually the first point of contact for customers. Their impact on customer satisfaction is typically disproportionate to their position and level of influence within the organisation. For many customers, customer service is a personal experience and depends significantly on the member of staff dealing with the customer at that particular time.

It is important that all customer-facing staff are trained in and are encouraged to apply customer care techniques. American service is often based on the ability of individual members of staff to provide individual service to customers. For example, all Wal-Mart associates wear an apron that reads 'How may I help you?' and are encouraged to greet customers when they are less that ten feet away. Wal-Mart associates understand that the customers matter.

There are a number of key points that organisations should consider in order to improve customer care. These include:

- As much as possible, employ customer-facing staff who are naturally helpful and friendly.

- Make all customer-facing staff aware of the need to care about customers.

- Provide the relevant training in customer care skills and techniques. These should be tailored to functions, e.g. call centre staff should be trained in dealing with angry customers, dealing with customer enquiries at first point of contact (see case study on Northern Ireland Electricity, p.106).

- Communicate best practice ideas.

- Ensure that customer-facing staff have enough technical knowledge about the company's product and services to provide the customer with high-quality information. One of the things customers find most irritating is an ill-informed company representative.

- Make use of available technology.

3.3.1 An example of poor customer care

A few years ago, a man walked into the busy reception area of a large multinational organisation. No one came to his aid or asked what he wanted so he took a seat. After 30 minutes, he got up and walked out – with a potential £20m contract.

3.4   Key Summary Points

- The focus on customers is primarily a cultural consideration that will need to be facilitated by organisational changes
- Internal customers are an important part of the customer chain and the customer focus philosophy
- All employees that come into contact with customers should be aware of or trained in customer care techniques

3.5   Further Reading

Cook S. (2000). *Customer Care*. Kogan Page, London.

EFQM Model – www.efqm.org.

Industrial Society. (1995). *Customer Care*. Managing Best Practice Series, Industrial Society, London.

Johnston R. (2001). *Service Excellence = Reputation = Profit*. Institute of Customer Service, UK. Institute of Customer Service.

Kaplan R.S., Norton D.P. (1996). *The Balanced Scorecard*. Harvard Business School Press, Massachusetts.

4. CUSTOMER COMMUNICATION

4.1 Introduction

Communication is important not just to customer satisfaction but to all aspects of an organisation's business, including production, human resources and purchasing. In terms of customer satisfaction, all stages of the customer service cycle (e.g. pre-sales, production, delivery, NPD, after-sales) require some form of communication with customers. However, organisations traditionally focus disproportionately on pre-sales communication, thereby neglecting the massive gains that could be obtained by keeping constant communications with customers. Furthermore, many organisations fail to make use of the full range of communication channels open to them. The increasing appreciation of the importance of having co-ordinated communication with customers has led to many organisations developing a communications plan (see case study on Northern Ireland Electricity, p.106). This not only ensures that they have an organised approach to reaching their target audience but also encourages them to consider various ways of making contact.

4.2 Understanding Communications Channels

The three most common communication media are written, verbal and visual communication. Examples of these media types are shown in Table 4.I. It is important that the organisation understands the characteristics of each of these ways of communicating. Many organisations will find that their communications plan will be more complex than anticipated. This is because different factors, such as product, customer profiles, market and culture, will affect the media used to get the message across to customers and prospective customers. Furthermore, the nature of the information to be communicated (e.g. product updates, customer satisfaction surveys) will have an impact on the media used.

TABLE 4.I
Types of communication media

Written communication	Verbal communication	Visual communication
Newsletters	Conferences	Video conference
Letters	Telephone discussions	Demonstrations
Reports	Meetings	Video tapes
Magazines	Exhibitions	Exhibitions
Brochures	Product briefings	Television adverts
E-mail	Messages	Posters
Internet site	Television adverts	Newspaper adverts
Handbooks	Radio adverts	Roadshows
Product literature	Training courses	Internet site
Newspaper adverts	Audio/video tapes	
Fax broadcasting	Speeches	
	Internet site	
	Video conference	

Irrespective of which combination of media is used, the organisation should ensure that its communication not only focuses on increasing interaction with prospective customers but also maintains the relationship with current customers.

4.3   Communications Plan

To promote an effective, comprehensive and consistent approach to communicating with customers, it is important to develop a communications plan or strategy. In developing such a plan, the organisation needs to take into consideration its current performance and its overall communications objective. This will involve factors such as:

- Profiles of current, past and prospective customers
- Nature of information to be communicated to each type of customer
- Location of customers
- Special consideration for certain customer groups – culture, religion, language
- Overall objectives of communication
- Current methods of communication

- Effectiveness of current methods of communication
- Ownership/management of proposed communications plan
- Resources available for the plan
- Evaluation of effectiveness of proposed plan
- Other relevant factors (e.g. legislation, industry regulatory agreements)

Traditionally, most of the communication with customers tends to be marketing- or product-led. However, as organisations become more relationship- and loyalty-focused, they increasingly recognise the need to communicate with customers over a wider range of issues. Consequently, it not unlikely that any combination of the factors mentioned below is communicated with customers.

4.3.1 Corporate information

It is often important for key customers to know that they can rely on their suppliers to continue adding value and servicing their needs. Consequently, it will be helpful from time to time to let customers have an idea of the direction of your business and other relevant information (e.g. financial results, annual reports).

4.3.2 Satisfaction surveys

Carrying out customer satisfaction surveys is a good way of finding out what your customers think about your organisation and its products, services and people. It can also give an indication about the future direction of your customers' businesses and the market in general. In return, customers should be made aware of any changes or improvements made as a result of the exercise. This assures your customers that their views and comments are taken seriously and that the organisation is focused on satisfying its customers.

4.3.3 Product updates

Providing your customers with up-to-date information on your products and services enables them to consider ways in which you can add more value and consequently enhances your organisation's status as an innovative and stable supplier. It also informs the customer of your technical capabilities and may lead to mutually beneficial situations such as joint technical research or product development.

4.3.4 Review meetings and briefings

These apply mainly to key customers. Review meetings tend to focus on the organisation's performance as a supplier. Where a service level agreement is in place, a review meeting provides an opportunity to assess the actual performance against the expected performance and to identify any other shortcomings in product or service delivery. Review meetings may be held monthly, quarterly or annually, depending on the level at which they are held, volume of trade, service agreements and geographical distance.

Customer briefings tend to be less structured and could cover a range of topics, such as new product launches, promotions, investment programmes, key personnel changes, etc.

4.3.5 Direct marketing

This is probably the most common way of communicating with customers. It involves sending general or customised information to particular individuals or customers. This may be in the form of letters, brochures, special offers or invitations to corporate events.

4.4 Quality of Communication

It is important to get the message to customers over in the right way. It is quite common for potential customers to be put off by the quality of communication being presented by the supplier. The need to communicate in an attractive and customer-friendly way applies to all the communication methods mentioned earlier. Some of the factors that may be taken into consideration include the following:

4.4.1 Language

Research has shown that many UK organisations believe it is totally unnecessary to speak the customer's language, even though 30% of those surveyed had more than a fifth of their customer base outside the UK. If a company does considerable business in a foreign country, being able to converse in the local language (even if it is just basic niceties) may have a distinct advantage. This could be during negotiations, potential customers establishing initial contact through the switchboard, or just creating a more congenial atmosphere during meetings.

Furthermore, other written or verbal communication methods (as well as product instructions) may be presented in the customer's language. This promotes easier sales and utilisation of the products and services on offer.

4.4.2   Letters

All relevant staff should be trained to produce letters that would be easy for the customer to understand. Such letters should have a contact name and a direct telephone number, where possible. The organisation may also wish to set internal standards where responding to customers is concerned (e.g. all requests for quotations must be acknowledged within 12 hours and dispatched within 3 days).

4.4.3   Verbal enquiries

Where a customer has chosen to make contact on the telephone or in person, it is important that the person dealing with the customer acts competently. This may include considerations such as recording the facts and re-confirming with the customer, identifying him- or herself, not passing a customer around the organisation unnecessarily, and providing details of how the customer may proceed with the enquiry/order.

4.4.4   Presentation

Organisations should ensure that general communication material such as leaflets, questionnaires and brochures are well laid out and easy for customers to follow and understand, and that information is conveyed in a customer-friendly tone.

4.4.5   Managing expectations

Where possible, organisations should let customers know the level and quality of communication that can be expected. While implicit expectations can be generated (e.g. customers know you have a 6-monthly newsletter or your switchboard operators are always friendly and helpful), expectations may also be set pro-actively or as part of a service agreement. Setting up and maintaining expectations of quality is an important way of presenting the organisation as customer-friendly.

4.5   Managing Communications

For organisations that communicate continuously with customers and for those that have a communications plan, it is worth considering having some sort of management structure to the communications approach. Typical considerations, shown in Fig. 4.1, include the following:

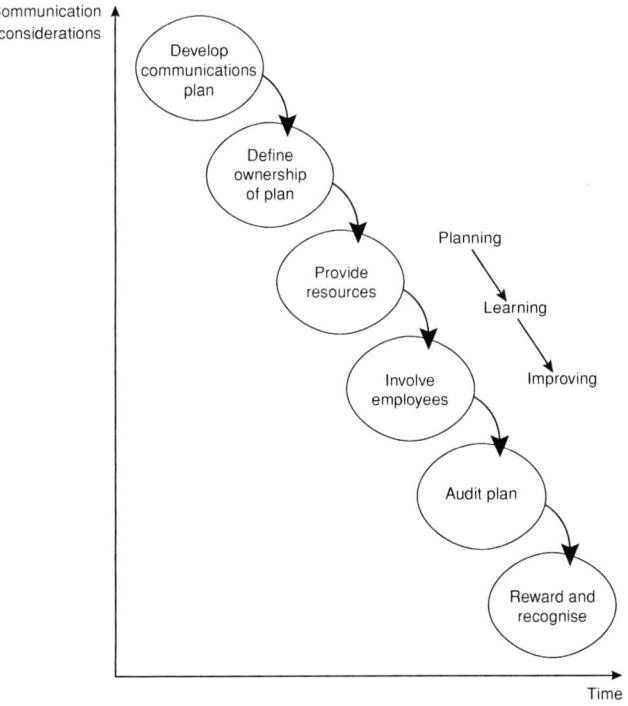

Fig. 4.1. Managing communications

4.5.1 Define ownership

It is important to promote good practice and collective ownership of customer communication among all employees at all levels. In addition, a director or senior manager may be given the responsibility for directly supporting and acting as mentor for the communications programme. Such a mentor will not only be a motivator but will also assist individuals and departments in the identification and fulfilment of customer requirements and promote an environment for an organisation-wide drive for customer focus.

4.5.2 Provide resources

A communications plan will inevitably require financial and other resources. These resources should be identified in some detail and made available as and when required by the plan. This would imply buy-in from the directors of the organisation. Overall responsibility for managing the resources may be handed to the mentor.

4.5.3 Involve employees

Employees should be involved not only in the development of the plan but also in the generation and nurturing of the practices to be directed at the customers. The communications plan and the company's expectations should be clear to and accepted by all those involved. This will help to further promote ownership.

4.5.4 Audit the plan

An audit of the communications plan and its results should be carried out to determine its effectiveness. To ensure robustness, any audits to be carried out should be pre-determined at the outset of the plan. At least two different kinds of audit can be carried out:

- An audit of the internal communications approach to identify issues to do with its management and adherence to expectations
- An audit of (a) particular client(s) to understand the customers' view of the business relationship and level of communication.

4.5.5 Reward and recognise

Rewarding and recognising excellent performance by staff helps to boost morale and provides a challenge for others within the organisation. It also sends a message that the organisation will reward the right behaviour. Increasingly, customers are being asked to identify staff who have provided a commendable level of service.

4.6 Key Summary Points

- Communication media are primarily classified into written, verbal and visual
- Organisations need to develop a suitable communications plan
- Develop and train employees to improve the quality of communications
- The communications plan needs to be managed formally

4.7 Further Reading

Stone M., Woodcock N., Machtynger L. (1997). *Customer Relationship Marketing*. Kogan Page, London.

5. BRANDED AND PRIVATE-LABEL PRODUCTS

5.1   Introduction

The food industry is one of the most brand-conscious industries worldwide. The very nature of food implies that most consumers are particular about what they eat and where they buy from. Traditionally, food products tended to be branded but, in the recent past, private-labels have provided strong competition, particularly for the cost-conscious consumer. There has been suggestion that increasing globalisation would favour the stronger brands. In this chapter, an examination of private and branded labels is presented and the relative merits and demerits of each examined.

5.2   Branded Products

Branding of products and services is a concept that extends well beyond the food industry to many aspects of our daily lives. While many consumers may claim to be rational enough not to be influenced by brand, a slightly closer examination will reveal that, in fact, individuals typically buy the same coffee, buy clothes from particular stores/designers, fly with particular airlines or use the same soap/toiletries.

Many organisations take the building and protection of their brand seriously, often going to great lengths and expense (including litigation) to define and promote their branded products and services. The way in which a brand is perceived by the customer can make or break an organisation. It is important that organisations realise that branding is much more than the façade of catchy slogans, distinct music and peculiar names that front many campaigns. It should be noted that the key reasons for creating brands include the following:

- A promise of a certain (or expected) quality of product or services. For example, a customer that flies with a particular airline or stays regularly in a particular group of hotels soon identifies an expected level of comfort or service. If such a customer is pleased with this service and the minimum standards expected are continuously met and exceeded, it may be difficult for a rival brand to successfully negotiate a defection.

- To create loyalty with the customer/consumer.

- To present a multinational/worldwide presence and consequently grow the organisation and generate instant customer/consumer recognition. Powerful consumer brands such as Coca-Cola are instantly recognised almost anywhere in the world. Even in markets where such products may not be currently available, there may be an awareness and a demand for them.

- To provide leverage against powerful retailers by exploiting loyalty/ familiarity with the end consumers. While retailers themselves are becoming powerful national and international brands, it is difficult to imagine a retailer having satisfied customers if it fails to stock popular brands such as Heinz, Campbell Soups and Colgate toothpaste, to mention a few.

- To differentiate a range of products from the same organisation. Organisations are constantly trying to develop new products, and having an established suite of tested and accepted products may mean that curious customers will anticipate a certain level of quality and will be willing to try the new products. Living up to the anticipated promise may lead to curious consumers becoming regular and loyal consumers.

5.2.1   Creating brands

There is no definitive way in which brands can be created. Some brands are based on a long history of defined and expected levels of quality while others are based on an ability to identify contemporary or anticipate future trends in consumer lifestyles (e.g. functional foods and health clubs). Furthermore, other brands are based on personalities with whom consumers associate (e.g. Richard Branson of Virgin Group and Stelios Haji-Ioannou of Easy Group). Irrespective of how a brand is developed, there are certain characteristics shared by most of the leading brands. The main ones are:

- Product and service attributes – this involves identification of the distinctive aspects or unique selling points of the organisation's offerings. These may be a combination of factors such as quality, cost, availability and volume.

- Target market – the organisation needs to identify the market for its particular range of offerings. This will be a combination of examining the attributes, the requirements of different sectors of the consumer base and the availability of competing products on the market. Factors that may be influential when considering the consumer will include spending power, age, lifestyle, culture and status. It is not uncommon for one organisation to have different brands targeted at different markets/consumers (e.g. Toyota Corporation produces both the Toyota brand and the more luxurious/expensive Lexus brand of cars).

- Marketing and awareness – this is the stage where the organisation addresses its target markets and creates/generates an expectation of a certain level of performance from its products or services. There are a number of well established ways (e.g. advertising, promotions, sponsorship) in which this can be achieved.

- Brand maintenance and integrity – having successfully established its brand, the organisation is duty-bound to maintain the levels of quality its customers have come to expect. They need to ensure that new products fit the established image. Furthermore, the organisation may find that other organisations try to exploit their success by manipulating consumer perceptions using similar product designs, logo, packaging, etc. It is not uncommon for such situations to lead to litigation in the effort to protect brand image.

5.3   Private-label Products

Traditionally, most manufacturers of branded products tend to view private-label products with some disdain. Reasons for this are not far-fetched – they are cheap, exploit the investment and success of branded products, make consumers more price-sensitive and enable already powerful retailers to become even more powerful. Private-label products have also been hugely successful and it is estimated that private-labels' market share in Europe in 1999 was more than 25% and growing.

The success of private-labels was given a massive boost when retailers started to market premium-quality private-label products. This was in direct competition to the branded products and the objective was to sell goods of comparable, or better quality at a slight discount. This new category of products was aimed at shoppers who were not overtly price-sensitive and would be willing to pay a little more for better-quality products.

For the consumer, the availability of value and premium labels has helped to improve satisfaction, if only because there is more choice and price competition. Retailers, who themselves are a brand, have also gained from the increasing penetration of their private-labels. Manufacturers, who are now forced into competing with their customers, the retailers, often see themselves in a more delicate position. Many of them produce private-labels for the retailers and, apart from the fact that they become 'invisible', they must also try to satisfy customers that also double as direct, and cheaper, competitors.

5.3.1 *Maintaining a balance between customer satisfaction and the 'labels war'*

All stakeholders in the food industry now accept that private-labels are here to stay. The challenge for brand-name manufacturers is to ensure customer satisfaction while viewing and exploiting private-labels as more of an opportunity than a threat. It is important to take note of the following, which apply, in particular, to premium private-labels:

- In a competitive market, supplying private-labels increases the overall market share of the manufacturer. This will also become advantageous in a market war against other leading brand-name competitors or market leaders.

- Retailers need manufacturers with established quality products and processes to supply premium private-label products. This generally implies that manufacturers may not have to commit extraordinary investment to supply private-labels of premium quality.

- While a shortcoming of supplying private-labels is that retailers can always change their source of supply, it more likely that they will stick with a manufacturer that is able to satisfy the contracted requirements. Difficulties faced in changing suppliers include cost outlay, possible need to change product recipe, packaging and established logistical practices.

- Premium private-labels will usually sell for less than brand names but, for the manufacturer, the margins are still higher than for the supply of value or traditional private-labels. There is also the added assurance of steady sales.

- Manufacturers that supply private-labels have advance awareness of retailer activity (e.g. promotions) and are able to adjust their strategy accordingly.

- It may be possible to develop new products in both brand-name and private-label markets by working with retailers on a partnership basis. This not only promotes teamwork and customer satisfaction, but also means that development cost and risk exposure are shared.

- Manufacturers can negotiate even higher margins when they have specialised or niche products.

- Supplying private-labels improves the trust and relationship between the supplier and the manufacturer and the retailer. This not only promotes mutual satisfaction but can be useful when other issues threaten to cause friction.

- Manufacturers have a choice of which private-label goods they produce and may choose not to supply private-label versions of their best-selling or market-leading products. For example, while Heinz makes both branded and private-label versions of many products, it will only make brand name ketchup.

The above arguments suggest that playing a key part in the private-labels market can have a lot of advantages for manufacturers. If they decide to become involved in the market, they need to see it not just as a sales opportunity but as a chance to improve customer relationships and satisfaction. However, brand name manufacturers must also ensure that they do not neglect their core branded business at the expense of private-label opportunities. They need to develop a long-term strategy of how they see their organisation evolving and decide on the policies that will lead this evolution.

5.3.2 Brand strategy options

Two of the key drivers of brand strategy are cost and loyalty. It is important to understand how this impacts on the organisation, its plans, customers and consumers. Figure 5.1 illustrates the key strategic options faced by organisations.

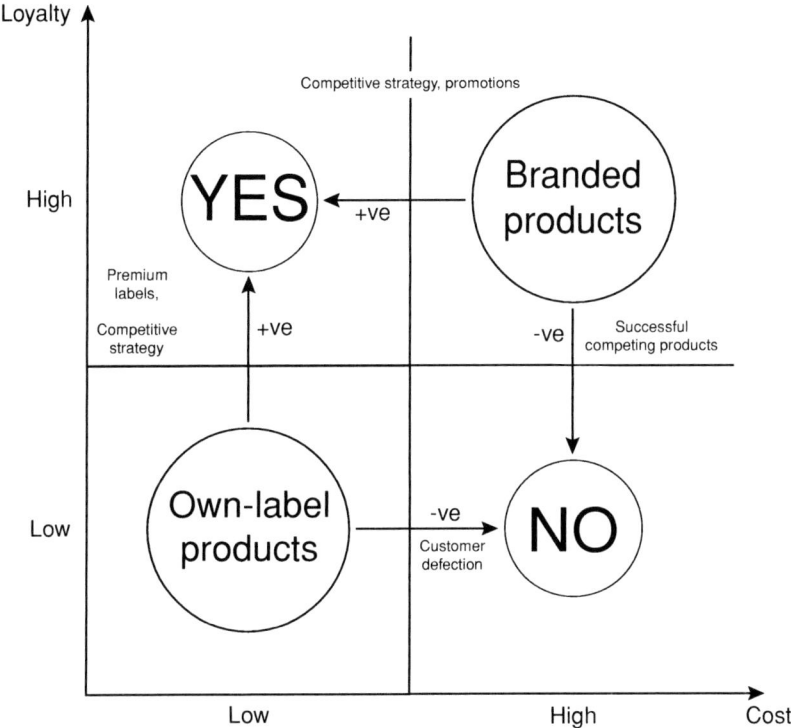

Fig. 5.1. Branding strategy analysis

5.4   Key Summary Points

- Creating a brand is an implicit promise to customers
- Maintaining brand attributes promotes customer loyalty
- Producing both branded and private-label products is a way to increase overall market share
- Manufacturers of private-label products need to develop pro-active relationships with retailers

5.5 Further Reading

Dunne D., Narasimhan C. (May/June 1999). The new appeal of private labels. *Harvard Business Review*, 41-52.

6. MANAGING CUSTOMER RELATIONSHIPS

6.1   Introduction

The dynamic nature of relationships between suppliers and their customers has been the subject of many studies in the recent past. A long time ago, suppliers (grocers, retailers, banks and car dealers) knew their customers individually and met their needs individually. As a result, long-term relationships and loyalty abounded. This nature of service came at a high cost to customers. Consumerism and the drive for efficiency-fuelled cost management meant that such individual service evolved into a culture of mass production; mass marketing reduced prices and limited the range of products and service.

It soon became apparent that many customers were not entirely satisfied with mass-produced goods and services as these did not always meet their specific needs. More recently, this has led to a re-focusing on customer requirements and the need to build relationships with customers. At first sight, this scenario might appear to be relevant only to organisations that deal with the general public, but business-to-business relationships have also gone through significant changes. Customers are increasingly moving away from having several suppliers of the same product to limited or even single sourcing. In the past, many businesses sourced goods by primarily focusing on price, but now other factors, such as quality, consistency, service level and added value play a key part in deciding the award of supplier contracts. This has implied that suppliers have been more proactive in developing positive relationships with their customers and working together on a win-win basis.

Technology is increasingly being used to good effect in the management of customer relationships. There is a wide variety of technological applications that enable organisations to manage all aspects of customer relationship – from marketing to post-sales communication.

6.1.1   On-line retailing

On-line retailing (alongside functional and organic foods) is one of the fastest growing sectors within the food industry. This growth industry brings new opportunities and threats to many organisations and would ultimately impact on customer relationships within the industry. There is the scope for new power battles to emerge. Traditionally, retailers have benefited from the power of aggregation (the ability to offer a range of products and services at one location) and the convenience this offers to consumers. On-line retailing now offers the following possibilities:

- The ability of smaller and more flexible aggregators to develop new relationships with traditional manufacturers and on-line shoppers. These relationships are likely to be driven by the provision of specialised products (in addition to traditional products) and services (faster delivery times that may facilitate convenience such as delivery to offices).

- The forming of on-line co-operatives and market places by major brand owners providing products and services to consumers and thereby by-passing traditional retailers. This could result in cheaper offerings to consumers, thereby altering the traditional dynamics of retail shopping. This model is already being practised in the airline industry, where a group of major international airlines now offers tickets direct to consumers from one Web site (opodo.co.uk).

6.2   Customer Relationship Types

6.2.1   Factors to be considered

In deciding which supplier to have a relationship with and the type of relationship to be fostered, customers can decide to use any combination of factors to assess their potential partner. The factors to be selected will typically support the strategic or operational practices of the customer. Most of the commonly used factors are grouped as follows:

6.2.1.1   Traditional factors in customer relationships

These factors include quality, cost, delivery, flexibility and lead time. In the recent past, many of these factors have practically become standard and may not necessarily form a strong basis for winning a supply contract. For example, the quality of food products acceptable to manufacturers, retailers and consumers is typically taken as a given and cannot be variable or inconsistent. Similarly, retailers typically define the time slot for deliveries and delivery lead times. Any organisation unable to satisfy these traditional factors is not likely to be on the shortlist for relationship development.

6.2.1.2   Innovation factors

Customers (e.g. retailers and top level manufacturers) are themselves in a very competitive market. In order to maintain competitiveness and increase market share, they constantly need to be innovative in the range of products and/or services they offer. A supplier that is innovative can add value to its businesses and consequently becomes a strong candidate for a long-term relationship. Innovativeness can be viewed in a number of ways, including novel applications (e.g. functional foods), presentation (new packaging methods) and service delivery (e.g. electronic ordering and invoicing).

6.2.1.3   Cultural factors

The development of a relationship suggests that both the customer and the supplier are compatible in non-technological ways. There is unlikely to be a sustained and mutually beneficial relationship between the parties if there are strong cultural differences. Cultural factors may include considerations such as management structure (command and control or empowerment), teamwork (ability/willingness to form joint improvement teams with the customer) and communication (is the supplier naturally communicative or fastidiously secretive and distant?).

6.2.1.4   Resource factors

As customers strive to improve their offerings in terms of range and flexibility, they need to know that they have a supplier with the requisite human and material resources to support a win-win growth strategy. At the very minimum, customers would expect their suppliers to invest sufficiently to ensure continuous operation and reliability of their (the supplier's) operational system. As an added advantage, customers will be more willing to form relationships with suppliers that are able and willing to invest in future growth (e.g. new production lines, R&D).

6.2.1.5   New business models

The development of technology is changing the way in which companies do business with their customers. This is leading to the development of new business models to fit with the new economy and its demands. The key attribute of these evolving business models is emphasis on service rather than just the product. For example, as manufacturers and retailers seek to reduce the need to hold excess stock, there is increasing pressure on their suppliers to align their product and service delivery with strategies such as just-in-time delivery and direct-to-store distribution. Consequently, suppliers are increasingly adopting new business practices such as lean production, agile production and cellular manufacturing.

6.2.2   Types of relationship

The factors described above, determine relationship types to a great extent. A study carried out at Politecnico di Milano classified key co-operative customer/suppliers relationships as explained below.

6.2.2.1   Type A (short-term logistic integration)

The primary focus of this type of relationship is the current manufacturing performance of the supplier. The customer often does not consider the future potential or resources of the supplier. The supplier is generally not regarded as a value-adding company and the customer can easily (and relatively cheaply) switch suppliers if a better supplier is found.

6.2.2.2   Type B (long-term logistic integration)

This involves more than just examining the current manufacturing performance and evaluating future potential for improvement. The assessment of future potential could involve the following:

- Identification of resources that will be important to the customer in future, e.g. a reduction in production cost could depend on new equipment, proper maintenance, new process technology and efficient production planning systems.
- The ability of the organisation to make these resources available when needed. This may involve more than just financial adequacy.

A relationship of this type will involve significant cost if the customer decides to change his source. This could be as a result of sunk and/or switching cost.

6.2.2.3   Type C (short-term strategic integration)

In this type of relationship, the customer views the supplier as both a manufacturer of the product and a source of technical expertise. The customer focuses on the current manufacturing and technical performance of the supplier. Future potential is not taken into account. Reasons why the relationship may be short-term will differ from case to case but, as an example, the supplier may own some new technological rights that might be of benefit to the customer's products but which the supplier might also be willing to promote to other customers. These relationships may also be as the result of a joint project under the terms of which each partner had decided to share the gains on successful completion.

6.2.2.4   Type D (long-term strategic integration)

This involves examining both the current and the future potential of the supplier. In addition, this assessment will encompass both the manufacturing and technological performance. This is probably the relationship that brings supplier and customer closest together. A breakdown of this type of relationship will involve significant costs for both parties.

*   *   *

The type of relationship developed between the supplier and the customer will depend on a range of factors, including those previously mentioned. What is important to note is that organisations that wish to be successful in the current competitive climate need to move away from a 'production business model' to an 'integrated business model'. Being successful with customers is no longer about trying to sell what the company produces but about producing what the customer wants. Integration goes further than just the products and includes the services, experience and people that delight customers. These form the building blocks of long-term relationships and enable suppliers to anticipate the needs of their customers.

6.3   Customer Lifetime Value

An understanding of the concept of customer lifetime value has helped several organisations understand the importance of maintaining long-term relationships with their customers. Customer lifetime value is the worth of a customer's business to you over the length of time that customer transacts business with your organisation. The likelihood is that the more the customers buy from you on a regular basis, the more they will be worth to you in terms of profitability.

Good businesses understand that losing a customer means they have potentially lost the lifetime value of that customer. In the short-term, it might make good business sense to accept a loss leader (investments, flexible arrangement, etc.) to realise value from a customer that has the potential of developing a long-term relationship. A customer who buys irregularly or as a stop-gap measure is unlikely to deliver solid value in the long term. Customers that deliver good lifetime value regularly buy a profitable product.

An often unappreciated relationship between customer relationships and lifetime value is that customers are in a position to significantly increase their lifetime value by purchasing other products from the supplier. For example, consumers that have developed a preference for or relationship with a certain food retailer brand now have the option of purchasing banking services, mortgages, clothes, etc., from that retailer, thereby increasing their lifetime value significantly.

6.4   Customer Relationship Management (CRM)

CRM is a new approach to managing customers. A recent survey sponsored by Sybase Business Intelligence showed that 90% of European Companies claimed to have a CRM strategy, although 50% of the companies were still at the planning stage of their CRM strategies. The CRM market was worth $9.4 billion in 1999 and is expected to rise to $34 billion in 2004.

6.4.1   What is CRM?

There is no common definition for the concept. Consequently, the understanding of CRM can differ quite noticeably from practitioner to practitioner. A working definition that will be used for the purposes of this book is as follows:

Activities a business performs to identify, qualify, acquire, develop and retain increasingly loyal and profitable customers by delivering the right product or service, to the right customer, through the right channel, at the right time and the right cost. CRM integrates sales, marketing, service, enterprise resource planning and supply chain functions through business process automation, technology solutions, and information resources to maximise each customer contact. CRM facilitates relationships among enterprises, their customers, business partners, suppliers and employees (Galbreath, 1999).

It is obvious that a lot of the confusion that has surrounded the understanding of the concept of CRM is the result of failure to understand what CRM is not and the adoption of a narrow view of the boundaries of the approach. The primary misconceptions are:

- CRM is using the right software to automate interactions with customers and, consequently, maximising sales potential.
- CRM is about the automation of service functions.
- CRM is about the automation of sales marketing and the supply chain.

While a successful CRM strategy will certainly involve elements of the above, they are not the overall focus of the concept. CRM is primarily about understanding customers and their needs by turning data and information into knowledge that enables the organisation to manage relationships better and treating the customers as individuals. CRM then involves managing this knowledge to provide individual solutions for customers across all functions (from product development through to delivery) of the organisation's business.

At a strategic level, CRM enables an organisation to identify who its key customers are, what they want and what their individual transactional preferences are. At an operational level, CRM automation enables tracking of customer contact (sales visits, complaints resolution, marketing opportunities, etc). The capabilities of CRM software packages differ from company to company and from operation to operation. Some packages enable the linking of front office (sales/customer contact) and back office (product development, production, delivery, etc) while others do not. CRM systems often support multiple channel relationship management – the customer should be able to contact you through a variety of communication channels and still have the details of their transactions dealt with at the first point of contact, even if a different channel is used each time.

6.4.2   e-CRM

The development of the Internet has changed the relationship between suppliers and customers – this is primarily manifested in the appearance of the 'virtual' customer. Whereas human contact, even by telephone, can facilitate gaining detailed insights into customers' wishes and frustrations and responding to them, how do you respond to a potential customer who is navigating your Web site helplessly?

Consequently, while the Internet offers great opportunities for attracting and developing relationships with customers, the traditional human contact for building the relationships is largely becoming virtual. e-CRM technologies focus on developing the 'online' customer relationship. However, this is still a growing industry and much of the currently available technology focuses primarily on optimising the functionality of online interactions with the customer.

In addition, there are e-CRM applications that support a variety of internal functions and activities aimed at improving customer relationships. For example, it is possible to create customer profiles (e.g. regularity of purchase, products purchased, cross-selling opportunities) that enable understanding the customer's business and habits and, hence the opportunity to add value to the customer's operations. Some of the available applications can help in predicting what customers want in terms of both product and service.

In developing an e-CRM strategy, there are a number of considerations that an organisation needs to take into account. A primary issue is that of linking the virtual customer with current operations or setting up a completely independent 'virtual' organisation. This is most commonly illustrated in the banking sector – while some banks have set up systems that enable customers to manage their 'bricks and mortar' account (thereafter called 'clicks and mortar') online, others have set completely new virtual 'Internet' banks (e.g. Smile, Egg, If).

Another key challenge of e-CRM will be the development of two-way communication. A lot of current models are configured to extract information from the customer without actually providing real-time feedback to the customer. Either software packages will have to become more sophisticated (particularly when determining customer preferences) or organisations will have to figure out another qualitative means of interacting with their customers.

What do managers need to do about CRM and eCRM in their organisations? The most important thing is to have a customer relationship strategy based on the key attributes of their products, service and customer expectations. The role that technology should play in the delivery of the strategy, if any, then needs to be evaluated and an implementation plan developed.

6.5   Personal Relationships

Traditionally, creating long-term relationships with customers often involves continual personal interaction. It has been suggested that the bonds of trust between a supplier and core customers are largely based on close, personal relationships between individuals in the company. While this is true of many market sectors, it is particularly true of the food industry, where there is a growing concentration of both buying and selling power.

The likelihood is that most food manufacturers in the UK will derive a sizeable proportion of their income from the biggest five retailers. Most will have personal contact with the buyer of the customers. Poor relationships between account managers and buyers have been known to be key sources of interface friction, while good relationships can be of benefit to both parties, particularly if the customer sources products from more than one supplier. As can be expected with personal relationships, there is no singular cause of bad relationships – differing company cultures, personal styles, personality types can all make the difference.

An important period in the development of these relationships is during the changeover of personnel. Even in cases where relationships have not been particularly satisfying, a changeover may prove a good opportunity to develop the relationship positively. To help with a positive handover, there are a number of issues to consider. These include:

- A full briefing on factors that are important to the buyer
- Assuring the customer of continuity of communication and co-operation
- A briefing on past problems with the customer and also the customer's procedures and structures.

6.6   Key Summary Points

- Customer relationships are affected by a range of factors that could be traditional, cultural, innovative, technological or resource enabled
- Customer relationship types need to be considered as part of the overall strategies of both the organisation and its customer
- A 'lifetime' relationship with customers is the best way to derive maximum value in the medium to long term.
- CRM is primarily a management approach facilitated with technological solutions (e-CRM)
- Personal relationships will continue to play a major role in the way organisations deal with customers

6.7   Further Reading

Anderson J.C., Narus J. (1998). Business marketing: understanding what customers value. *Harvard Business Review*, 53-65.

Galbreath J., Rogers T. (1999). Customer relationship leadership: a leadership and motivational model for the twenty-first century business. *The TQM Magazine*, 11 (3), 161-71.

Masella C., Rangone A. (2000). A contingent approach to the design of vendor selection systems for different types of co-operative customer/supplier relationships. *International Journal of Operations and Production Management*, 20 (1), 70-84.

Rigby D.K., Reichheld, F.F., Schefter P. (2002). Avoiding the four perils of CRM. *Harvard Business Review*, 101-9.

7. CUSTOMER SERVICE

7.1   Introduction

With increasing globalisation and customer power in the food industry, it is now accepted that a product is no longer enough to keep suppliers competitive. In many instances, different manufacturers can supply a retailer with a product made to specification. The services offered with the product can, however, make a difference in the customer's perception of the supplier and lead to increased customer satisfaction (or dissatisfaction).

7.2   'Service' Attributes

Traditionally, the food industry has been 'product'-oriented – the only important thing was getting the product to the customer. However, the industry has become more sophisticated and, as retailers pay more attention to issues such as supply chains, lead times and order fulfilment, it has become vital for manufacturers to improve their service performance. Some of the key factors to consider with respect to service are described as follows:

- *You are only as good as your last performance* – Retailers (and other customers) often run very dynamic businesses and consequently have dynamic demands of their suppliers. The supplier's performance must therefore continually change to meet minimum acceptable levels of service.
- *Customers compare service performance* – Customers will often compare actual service delivery with their expectations. These expectations can be based on a number of factors, including past performance and competitor performance. The gap between expectation and delivery will help determine the customer's appreciation of the service.

- *Customers don't always express their service needs or expectations* – While customers generally stipulate, in at least reasonable detail, the characteristics or attributes of the product(s) they require, it is less common to do the same for service attributes. In some cases, less sophisticated customers might not know what their exact needs or problems are, while more advanced customers may specify requirements through service level agreements (SLAs). Typically, SLAs are agreed when product supply contracts are negotiated and sometimes leave room for re-evaluation or re-negotiation (e.g. during special events such as promotions or opening of new consumer outlets).

- *Suppliers and customers depend on each other to optimise service delivery* – In the food sector, as in many other sectors, the customer greatly controls the balance of power. It is however, in their interest to work closely with their supplier(s) to ensure that the delivery of service suits both parties, as poor service from manufacturers will ultimately impact on the service performance to the end consumer. Thus customers and suppliers must continuously work together both to define service specifications and to resolve any problems that arise.

- *People deliver service* – The successful delivery of service is very people-dependent. Whether it is order-taking, delivering products or invoicing, performance depends greatly on the abilities and motivation of the individuals involved. The mechanistic tools that are applicable on the production shop floor may not make much of an impact when it comes to managing service delivery. It is therefore important that organisations invest in their 'outwards-facing' people.

- *Different industries have different drivers* – The key drivers of value-adding service differ from industry to industry and from customer to customer. Some customers may have preferences for delivery performance while other may prefer improved communication. It is important to understand the services that impact most on the customers that the organisation services.

7.3   Understanding Service Needs

The realisation that service needs differ from customer to customer (or for different customer types) implies that suppliers that wish to maintain a competitive edge must make extra efforts to understand their customers' service needs in addition to product requirements. There are a number of approaches to providing service that delights customers, including the following.

- Ask the customers – By directly asking individual customers or groups of customers what their service needs are, the supplier can tailor its resources to meet those requirements. Customer research methods such as telephone and face-to-face interviews as well as questionnaires are very useful for this approach.
- Re-define expectations – Re-defining the expectations that customers have of not just your company but of the industry can result in customer delight. Service offerings of this nature are usually identified by the supplier to provide added value for the customer and thus lead to satisfaction and even market gain. A good example of the redefinition of expectations is in the car industry, where some of the less expensive brands offer add-ons such as free service, breakdown cover, insurance and car finance in one package.
- Learn from others – By observing what competitors and even organisations from outside the industry offer, a new understanding of services that may be beneficial to customers may be gained. It is however, important that the principles behind such offerings are understood and applied to the company's own products and customers rather than the company simply attempting to copy what others are doing.

From the application of the above approaches, it is often possible to identify different types of customers and their service needs. As an example, Otis lifts identified its customer types and their relevant critical success factors. While these segments may not be particularly relevant to the food manufacturing industry, they give an insight into approaches that companies in the food sector might consider for their own operations. The four customer types or 'segments' identified by Otis are described below.

7.4   Identified Customer Types

7.4.1   'At all costs'

These are customers to whom consistent and high-quality service is a must. They are willing to pay a premium for peace of mind. Safety and reliability are also high on the list of service needs. Critical success factors for this class of customer include quick solutions and senior management availability.

7.4.2 *'Service at a price'*

These tend to be 'value for money' companies. They have specified minimum standards for service but keep an eye on the cost. One of their key drivers is product availability, but with 'invisible' service. Critical success factors include price and response time.

7.4.3 *'Interested, but no leverage'*

These are customers that are interested in performance, although it does not impact greatly on their business. The main drivers and critical success factors are low cost, swift response time and visible service.

7.4.4 *'Necessary evil'*

These are the budget or bucket shop customers. They want the cheapest deal, and performance and quality of service are not a consideration. The critical success factors for this type of customer are lowest cost and an ability to reduce cost while not reducing perceived service.

* * *

The identification of these customer types enabled the company to provide service packages that were specifically suited to customer needs. Different contracts were drawn up to support the different levels of commitment. Furthermore, processes and technologies appropriate to each contract type were identified and staff were re-trained.

7.5   Customer Service and Technology

The growth in appreciation of the importance of customer service has been shadowed by the growth in development and application of technology for improving service performance. For almost all aspects of customer service and interaction, ranging from order taking through market research to after-sales support, there are technological tools to facilitate ease of the process. Some of these are familiar technologies with new applications while others are relatively new tools. A few applications of technologies are now briefly discussed below.

7.5.1 Technology applications

7.5.5.1 The telephone

The telephone continues to be one of the most versatile tools applicable in customer service. The number of applications of the telephone has grown considerably, to include service aspects such as order taking, telephone research, telemarketing, helplines and database support.

7.5.5.2 Software

Knowledge management, customer intelligence and CRM database software are increasingly playing important roles in customer service. By storing customer and transaction information in a central store from which it can be retrieved by a number of people, customer history is immediately available, the progress of goods through the supply chain is easily visible and customer needs can often be addressed at the first point of contact. For example, CRM applications improve customer visibility throughout the organisation – different people in different departments have access to all information known about the customer without necessarily having to ask directly from other departments. In addition to improving service, operational and cost benefits are derived by the service provider.

7.5.5.3 e-Service

More recently, Internet and e-service applications have provided new opportunities for improving customer service. Business and private customers now have opportunities to browse products, make enquiries and purchase products online. This may be particularly useful if a potential customer is on the other side of the world. Within manufacturing operations, customer orders, production plans, raw material inventories and suppliers at a single site or across the world can now be linked. Through the use of portable computers and Wireless

Application Protocol (WAP), field-based service agents can have instant access to head-office mainframes, thereby speeding up response time and reducing unnecessary travel and its associated costs. Where product delivery service is concerned, improvements in telematics implies that a transport or distribution manager can know the exact location and speed of a goods consignment and give an angry or anxious customer a fairly accurate arrival time window.

7.6 Customer Service Frameworks

There are a number of frameworks in use that assist organisations to improve their levels of customer service and focus. Two of the most widely known ones are SERVQUAL (service quality) and Efficient Consumer Response (ECR).

7.6.1 SERVQUAL

This framework is widely used for measuring service quality. It has been applied across a wide range of sectors, including the manufacturing, public and voluntary sectors. SERVQUAL identifies ten key service attributes that organisations should focus on and measure. These are:

i) Reliability: the ability to provide what was promised – dependably and accurately.

ii) Assurance (credibility, security, competence, courtesy) – the knowledge and courtesy of employees and their ability to convey trust and confidence.

iii) Tangibles: the physical facilities – equipment, premises, the appearance of personnel, appearance of documentation and communication materials.

iv) Empathy (communication, access, understanding the customer) – the degree of caring and individual attention provided to customers; a complete understanding of the needs of the customer.

v) Responsiveness: the willingness to help customers and provide prompt service.

vi) Communication: presentation about the service – explaining what is to be delivered, how much it will cost, how problems will be handled, etc.

vii) Credibility: trustworthiness, believability and honesty – company name and reputation, personal characteristics of contact personnel.

viii) Security: freedom from danger, risk or doubt – physical safety, financial security or confidentiality.

ix) Competence: possession of the required skills and knowledge to perform the service.

x) Access: approachability and ease of contact – convenient hours of operation and location of facility.

SERVQUAL has a number of positive attributes and key uses. These include measuring a wide range of factors that impact on the customer. Commendably, some of these factors are 'soft' measures (e.g. empathy, responsiveness and credibility), which are often difficult to evaluate even though they impact significantly on customers.

However, it is important to note that SERVQUAL is only one tool and should be used in conjunction with other improvement tools. In particular, being a measurement tool, it gives an idea of performance metrics, but a knowledge of performance metrics in themselves is not of much use if they are not used as input into a programme of continuous improvement.

7.6.2   ECR (efficient consumer response)

ECR focuses primarily on supply chain performance. It aims to improve the quality and effectiveness of links in the chain by focusing on the flow of products from factory to consumer and the flow of data and information in the opposite direction. ECR uses a scorecard approach to determine the status of implementation of 14 concepts (Fig. 7.1) that constitute the framework.

These concepts are:

- Strategy and capabilities
- Optimising assortments
- Optimising introductions
- Optimising promotions
- Continuous replenishment
- Automated store ordering
- Synchronised production
- Integrated suppliers

CUSTOMER SATISFACTION

- Reliable operations
- Electronic data interchange (EDI)
- Electronic funds transfer (EFT)
- Cross-docking
- Activity-based costing
- Item coding and database management.

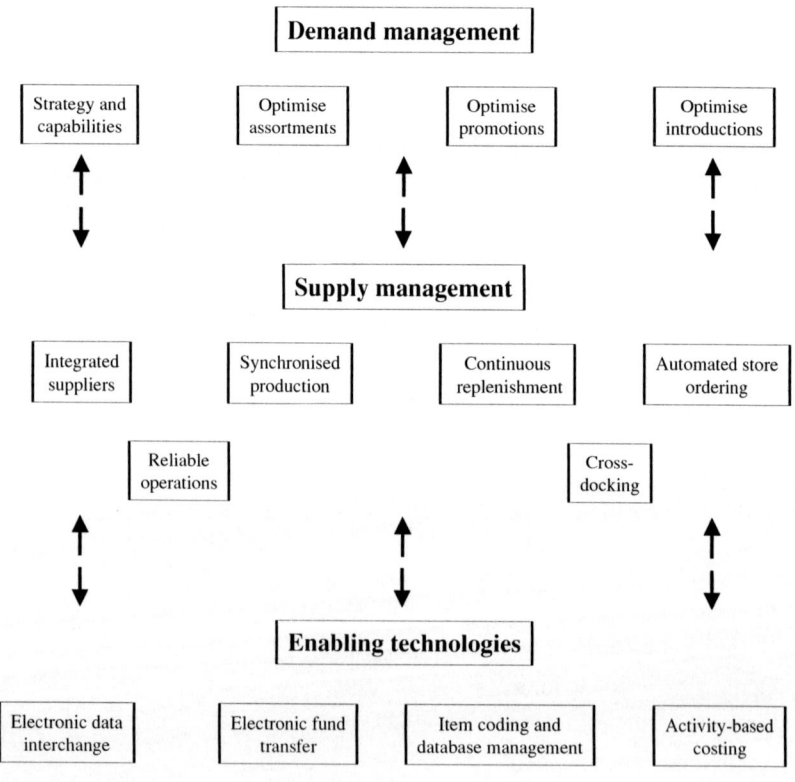

Fig. 7.1. ECR improvement concepts

Two of the strategic advantages of ECR are that it facilitates common understanding between companies in the supply chain and that it can act as an industry-wide tool to identify areas for general improvement. However, it is important to note ECR is primarily systems-oriented. It is primarily about putting in place techniques and technologies to optimise processes and mainly achieve the hygiene factors mentioned in Chapter 2 and in the BT case study.

ECR does not focus on the 'soft' issues that are more characteristic of SERVQUAL. There is also a belief that ECR is oriented towards retailers. Within the UK food industry, ECR has been widely promoted by the Institute of Grocery Distribution (IGD).

7.6.3   The supply chain perspective

The financial savings and operational benefits that can be derived from having a supply chain infrastructure that is complementary to a manufacturer's strategic and operational attributes and their product types have led to an increased focus on the interrelationships between these factors. Marshall Fisher illustrated these relationships by classifying supply chains as either responsive or efficient and products as either functional (e.g. soup) or innovative (e.g. ski-wear). A modified Fisher diagram has been developed at the University of Liverpool Management School and is shown in Fig. 7.2.

7.7   Key Summary Points

- Customer service is unique to each customer
- Service performance can be improved through understanding and partnership with customers
- Technology should be fully exploited to improve service performance
- Customer service frameworks provide a tool to facilitate service delivery improvement

7.8   Further Reading

Contact organisation – Institute of Grocery Distribution (IGD). www.IGD.co.uk.

Fisher M. (1997). What is the right supply chain for your product. *Harvard Business Review*, 105-16.

Johnston R. (2001). *Service Excellence = Reputation = Profit.* Institute of Customer Service, UK.

Parasuraman A., Zeithami V., Berry L.L. (1986). *Servqual: A multiple-Item Scale for Measuring Customer Perceptions of Service Quality.* Marketing Science Institute.

Romeijn A. (1999). How to produce better service. *Measuring Business Excellence.* 3 (2), 16-21.

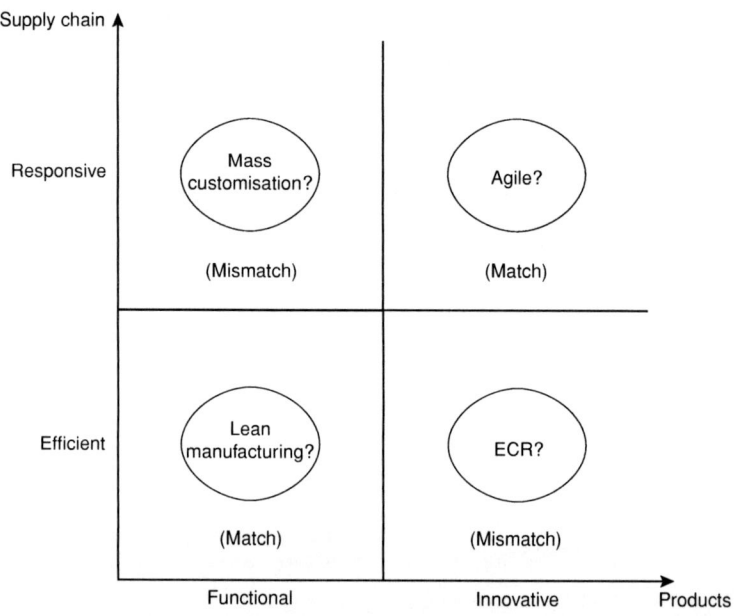

Source: University of Liverpool Management School

Fig. 7.2. Modified Fisher diagram of supply chain classification (original Fisher classification in parentheses)

8. CUSTOMER LOYALTY AND RETENTION

8.1　Introduction

Until the early 1990s, the concept of customer loyalty was not well understood. It was largely believed that loyalty was more or less a by-product of customer satisfaction. It is now known and accepted that, while customer satisfaction is necessary for any successful business, it is not enough to guarantee loyalty. Frederick Reichheld, the leading international expert on loyalty, found that between 65 and 85% of customers who said they were satisfied or very satisfied with their former supplier had switched to a different supplier. Reichheld also found that, on average, US corporations lost half their customers every 5 years. This chapter examines the concept of customer loyalty and reviews some of the work that has been done on the subject.

8.2　Why Customer Loyalty?

The importance of customer loyalty is being understood and accepted by more and more organisations in different sectors. Many organisations have even set up schemes to reward 'loyalty' – e.g. frequent flyer miles and grocery store reward programmes. But why do organisations go to great lengths to try to keep their customers? Some reasons are more widely known than others, but the key ones are as follows:

- It is easier and more cost-effective to retain current customers than to attract new ones. Many organisations base their strategies on increasing their market share primarily by gaining new customers. Unfortunately, they do not always put in enough effort to retain their existing client base, therefore making the attainment of their market share objective even more difficult. Table 8.I highlights the differences between market share and customer loyalty strategies.

- It is easier to sell to existing customers. Existing customers have already accepted your products and generally will not need the same amount of sales effort that prospective customers will. This may be particularly important when trying to cross-sell other products or launching new products.

- There is a strong causal relationship between loyalty and profit and cash flow. With respect to profits, the general rule is that the longer a customer stays loyal, the better the profits for the company. The benefits of loyalty are even more prominent in the generation of cash flow, particularly for business-to-business relationships in relatively 'stable' sectors such as the food industry.

- Loyalty promotes trust and leads to even better relationships. An organisation's customers are typically in competitive markets themselves and, to stay ahead, they often have to be innovative and/or flexible. In developing new products, for example, they are more likely to involve a supplier with whom they have a trusting and long-standing relationship and whose capability, technology, performance and people they are sure of.

- Companies with loyal customers tend to grow faster. There are a number of reasons for this, including the fact that they do not need to spend over the odds to maintain/increase their market share. Consequently, their resources can be spent on other developmental issues.

- There is a strong relationship between loyalty and branding. A consequence of this is that customers that are loyal to a brand are more willing to pay a premium for products, thus increasing margins and generating growth for the company.

- There is a fairly well defined link between loyal customers and loyal people. Personal relationships developed between customer and supplier representatives mean that employees generally tend to find it easier to deal with existing customers. Customers are also more likely to be reliant on the opinion of a supplier representative in whom they have developed trust. The overall effect is that the customer receives better service while the employee is more likely to enjoy the job, stay with the company and reduce the potential for upheaval related to switching jobs – i.e. cost of recruiting, establishing new relationships and losing current customers to defecting sales staff.

• Loyal customers are more likely to tell others about your company and its products.

TABLE 8.I
Market share vs loyalty

	Market share strategy	Loyalty strategy
Goal	Buyer switching	Buyer loyalty
Market condition	Low-growth or saturated markets	Low-growth or saturated markets
Focal point	Competition	Customers
Measure of success	Share of market relative to competition	Share of customer Customer retention rate

Source: Griffin, 1997

8.3   What is Customer Loyalty?

Defining a loyal customer is probably not as easy as it first seems. Is a customer that keeps buying from you but moves some of his purchases to another supplier still a loyal customer? What about the buyer that buys more from you but whose transactions with your company is a lesser proportion of overall increased spends. Before classifying customers, it would be useful to try to understand some of the behaviours a supplier would expect from a loyal customer and what makes customers loyal.

If customer satisfaction is necessary but not enough to build loyalty, what factors are important to make customers loyal? There is a significant acceptance that value is the most important factor in promoting customer loyalty. Suppliers must see themselves as not just deliverers of products but deliverers of added value to the customer's business. Customers will identify added value in terms of factors that would improve their own business performance – cost, time, flexibility, quality, etc. The supplier needs to make sure that the products and services given to the customer reflect the attributes that the customer values (see Fig. 8.1).

Perhaps more importantly, customers would compare the value a supplier gives with the value they would get or expect to get from a competing supplier. If the perceived value from a competitor is greater, then the customer, even if satisfied with past service, is likely to strongly consider a defection to the higher-value supplier.

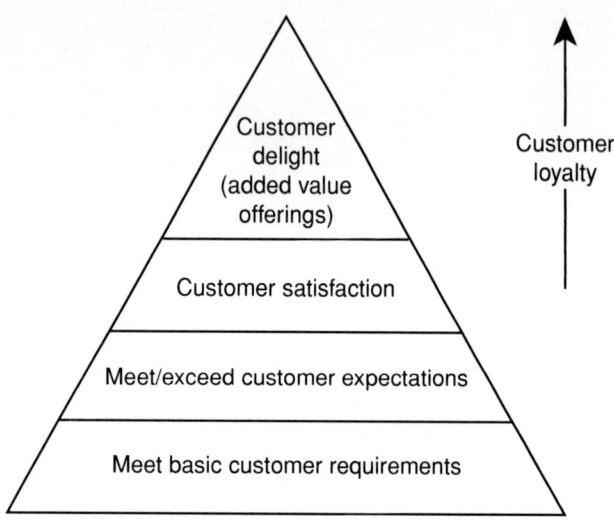

Fig. 8.1. The route to customer loyalty?

8.3.1 *Behaviour of loyal customers*

Loyal customers will typically have certain behaviours or characteristics that differentiate them from other customers. It is worth noting that not all loyal customers will exhibit all of the behaviours, but it is reasonable to expect the majority of certain 'core' behaviours from them. The suggested 'core' behaviours are:

- buying routinely (and increasingly) from the supplier
- recommending the supplier to others
- favouring the supplier's products over those of competitors
- informing the supplier about problems/shortcomings
- buying, where applicable, a range of products/services from the supplier's portfolio.

In addition to these, loyal customers may exhibit some of the following 'non-core' behaviours:

- single sourcing from the supplier
- making the supplier their first point of contact for information or product enquiries
- honouring invoices on time
- informing the supplier automatically of any changes or anticipated changes in their requirements
- recognising good supplier performance
- maintaining a relationship with the supplier
- re-aligning purchase processes to promote ease of transaction and added value for both parties.

These behaviours are not, in themselves, exclusive to loyal customers. What differentiates loyal customers is the fact that they are likely to exhibit most of these behaviours and, in particular, the core behaviours.

8.4   Classifying Loyal Customers

In order to classify loyalty, it is important to understand the relationship between the product and the customer's attitude or preference for the product. This relationship is shown in Table 8.II. The indication is that customers have higher levels of attachment where a supplier's product can be differentiated from the competition. This attachment is highest where a customer has a strong preference for the product type, e.g. a consumer may have a strong preference for wheat-based breakfast cereals and then go on to differentiate the various wheat-based cereals on the market. Higher attachment is likely to lead to greater loyalty.

TABLE 8.II
Customer attachments to products

Customer attitude	Product differentiation	
	No	Yes
Strong	Low relative attitude or attachment	Highest relative attitude or attachment
Weak	Lowest relative attitude or attachment	High relative attitude or attachment

In contrast, a customer is likely to have least attraction where there is no product differentiation and where there is not a strong preference for the product type. This is the case with products that are commoditised or seen to be so. This is likely to lead to poor loyalty.

Branding (e.g. Levi's/gap jeans) and partnership (e.g. Shell) are key strategies aimed at escaping commoditisation.

The relationship between the level of attachment and the purchase habits of the customer enables the identification of the type of loyalty exhibited. There are primarily four types of loyalty, as shown in Table 8.III. As may be expected, the highest level of loyalty occurs when the customer feels highly attached to the product and repeatedly buys from the supplier. The opposite is true of the worst case scenario – no loyalty.

TABLE 8.III
Types of loyalty

Relative attitude	Repeat purchase	
	Low	High
High	Latent loyalty	Premium loyalty
Low	No loyalty	Spurious (or inertia) loyalty

8.5 Why Companies Fail to Achieve Customer Loyalty

A low level of attachment accompanied by a high level of repeat purchase is indicative of 'spurious' or 'inertia' loyalty. This is the case when a customer buys for situational reasons, e.g. convenience or interpersonal reasons. Situational factors are also likely to be the cause of 'latent' loyalty. This is characterised by a high relative attitude and low repeat purchase.

Understanding this relationship can help companies further improve the loyalty of their customers. By investigating the situational factors that cause 'spurious' or 'latent' loyalty, steps can be taken either to build on the strengths or to improve on the weaknesses that reduce the customer's value to the supplier.

The drive for customer satisfaction in the '80s encouraged many organisations to set up customer-focused programmes. This investment, however, has not enabled all companies to reduce their customer defection significantly and progress from customer satisfaction to customer loyalty. There are a number of reasons that have been suggested for this, including the following:

- Companies adopt a philosophy and, hence, a culture of making and selling products, rather than a culture of developing loyal and repeat purchase customers.

- Many companies do not fully understand the relationship between customer loyalty and cash flow, profits and lifetime value. Projected cash flow and profits of long-term loyalty cannot be captured by accounting systems geared towards short-term measures.

- Companies spend a lot of effort and resources on acquiring new customers and thereafter fail to monitor their performance, level of customer satisfaction and likelihood to defect. Customer loyalty is probably most delicate immediately after a switch of supplier. Inability to deliver and add the expected value means that they defect to another supplier or even go back to their old supplier.

- The reasons for customer defection are not always investigated and understood. Companies and individuals might feel vulnerable and uncomfortable studying failure.

- Companies sometimes target the wrong type of customer. It is important to know the customers for whom the company and its products provide added value and who are more likely to remain loyal. Customers who can get better value elsewhere are unlikely to become repeat buyers.

- Customer defection is sometimes difficult to identify, particularly if the customer transfers only a proportion of its business or buys less frequently.

- Companies do not always develop relationships with key players in the customer's organisation. This often means that they are unaware of the customer's future purchase intentions and any problems that the customer may be having with products and services.

- Companies tend to focus their growth programmes on factors such as new products, cost rationalisation and new customers, while paying, in contrast, little effort to the customers they already have.

- The importance of having loyal customers and the consequent repeat purchases is not always understood by people that work for the supplier. Consequently, their actions and behaviours may not be reflective or supportive of this ideal.

These reasons for failure to reduce customer defection suggest that companies need to understand the importance of customer loyalty, educate their people and put in place systems that would encourage high-value customers to maintain their patronage. This would involve training of staff and an understanding of the customers. Database analysis and market research can identify current and potential customers that would deliver long-term value to the organisation in terms of purchase intentions and inter-company process integration. eCRM applications can also be useful in identifying high-value customers.

When such customers have been identified, the company needs to engage actively in dialogue to understand the factors that would make them the 'ideal' supplier to each key customer. It is increasingly obvious that high-value customers look beyond just financial considerations in dealing with their suppliers. Loyalty is increasingly becoming dependent on factors such as service performance, understanding of and value added to customer's business, partnership and technical capabilities.

8.6   Key Summary Points

- Loyal customers are the most valuable customers an organisation can have
- Loyal customers are of different types and need to be managed differently
- The value (or perceived value) that customers derive from products and services is a key driver of satisfaction
- Customer loyalty should play a prominent role in an organisation's development strategy

8.7   Further Reading

Bhote K.R. (2000). *The Customer Loyalty Audit.* Pearson Education, London.

Griffin J. (1997). *Customer Loyalty,* Jossey-Bass, San Francisco.

Reichheld F.F. (1996). Learning from customer defections. *Harvard Business Review*, 56-69.

Reichheld F.F., Schefter P. (2000). E-Loyalty: your secret weapon on the web. *Harvard Business Review*, 78 (4), 105-13.

9. CUSTOMER COMPLAINTS

9.1 Introduction

A study by the Institute of Customer Service and TMI (training consultants) in 2001 found that the trend for complaining was rising, with 50% of respondents complaining most or all of the time. The study also indicated high expectations from complaining customers – 55% of people who complain in person and over 50% of people who complain over the phone expect same day resolution. Furthermore, organisations still fail to exploit the full opportunity that a complaint represents in terms of improving customer relationships. The study also indicated a cultural reluctance to deal with complaints because organisational behaviours were divergent from the company's stated customer service values. This chapter examines the subject of customer complaints in some depth in order to give readers an informed view of why organisations should take complaints with more than just a pinch of salt.

9.2 The Nature of Complaints

There is an acceptance that society is becoming better at complaining even though many companies claim that customer service, buoyed by technology, has become better and better. Have customers become more discerning in their expectations or is society simply becoming rude? How should companies view complaints and complaining customers?

9.2.1 Why complaints?

Customers tend to complain when products and service quality or attributes fall below requirements or expectations. While a tiny proportion of customers may have expectations that are near impossible to satisfy, the majority of customers would base their expectations on agreed specifications, previous experience or comparability to the performance of competing organisations or products. The likelihood that customer expectations are far-fetched is likely to be even lower when dealing with other companies than when dealing with the general public.

There has been plenty of research to show that the majority of customers who either have a problem or are dissatisfied do not complain to the company but tell other customers or potential customers and then quietly move their business elsewhere. Ironically, it then appears that some of the customers that complain are actually loyal customers who feel let down and would like the supplier to put things right. Companies should take complaints seriously for reasons that include the following:

- One customer complaint is indicative that there may be a lot of other customers that have not complained.

- Complaints are indicative of dissatisfied customers. Failure to address complaints adequately could lead to defection of customers.

- Complaints provide information on where the company's processes have gone wrong.

- Speedy resolution of complaints can actually make potential defecting customers become more loyal. An American study has estimated that a speedy response can increase customer loyalty by up to 25%. Furthermore, such customers are more likely to tell other potential customers about the efficient resolution of their complaints.

- Identifying and eliminating the causes of complaints reduce the likelihood of such complaints in the future, thereby saving money and time required to address the complaints.

- Addressing and resolving complaints have a positive impact on employee morale and levels of job satisfaction.

The awareness and benefits of customer complaints are so important that best practice companies make it easy for their customers to complain. They see this as an expedient way to improve their business and its performance since customers are probably the first to know when things are not working.

9.2.2   Challenges faced by suppliers

The indicated performance of UK companies with respect to managing customer complaints does raise questions about the effectiveness of the various customer satisfaction processes put in place. Why do companies still fail to manage complaints well when many claim to understand the importance of and have spent a lot of money on customer care programmes? The challenges, obviously, vary from company to company but the most common ones are as follows:

- Empowerment – many employees are not empowered to resolve customer complaints. This often means that complaints cannot be resolved at the first point of contact, resulting in poor morale, customer dissatisfaction and increased cost of tracking and resolving complaints.

- Efficiency – customers often want a quick resolution to their complaints. Even where, for operational or other reasons, complaints cannot be resolved at the first point of contact, customers will want to know that the problem will be resolved as soon as possible and that the company will contact them (see case study Λ on Pernod Ricard).

- Process management – poor development and management of the customer complaints process may lead to poor tracking and even loss of customer complaints. Furthermore, weak systems may mean that not all complaints are recorded, e.g. where expressed verbally to salesmen on site visits.

- Customer service skills – some companies do not train their employees in ways of dealing with complaining or dissatisfied customers. Even where systems are in place to deal with problems, frontline employees need to be aware and skilful in 'softer' attributes such as listening, asking the right questions, empathising, calming irate customers and keeping calm.

- Commitment – management commitment to resolving customer complaints is sometimes weak. There is a danger that resolving customer complaints is seen as a nuisance or, at best, a necessary evil rather than a key opportunity to improve customer satisfaction and loyalty.

- Measurement – failure to establish proper measurement systems may mean that companies do not know how their customer complaints process is performing and what needs to be improved. Without such systems, it would be difficult, if not impossible, to have vital information such as how long it takes to resolve complaints and what it costs the organisation. Emerging metrics in complaints measurement include measurements of how well complaints were handled and measures of how often service fails in relation to complaints received.

9.3 Pro-active Complaints Management

To improve levels of customer satisfaction and loyalty, companies need to be more pro-active in the way they manage their complaints. They also need to have robust systems in place to manage both small-scale and large-scale incidents of customer complaints. Two important areas are those of product recall and data management.

9.3.1 Product recall

Product recalls do not happen regularly. However, they tend to be quite serious incidents when they do occur and they are probably one of the worst results that could emerge from a customer complaint. This is because many product recalls involve products that are or could potentially be a danger to health or life. Consequently, these products need to be located and removed from the market as soon as possible.

While the nature of the food industry makes it susceptible to product recalls, once potential danger is identified, there are probably similar if not greater risks in other industries, such as the automotive, electrical goods and household goods industries. There are two common ways in which product recalls are triggered:

- Customer complaint/experience – customers that experience problems during regular use of the product complain of the hazard or potential hazard faced. Where this is a one-off or manageable situation, a product recall may not be necessary, but where there is a system error (e.g. defect in brake design of a car or a dangerous batch of contaminants in food), a recall may be inevitable.

- Internal inspection/testing – non-conformances may be found as a result of internal inspection or testing. It is possible that some of the potentially hazardous product is already in use by customers who may or may not have experienced problems from using the product.

The fact that large-scale product recalls could be initiated by one or a few customer complaints is another reason why companies must take customer complaints seriously and investigate them quickly and thoroughly.

Experience has shown that most problems that lead to product recalls are due to system and/or human error. However, there have also been a few cases of products having been defective as a result of sabotage. It is important that customer complaints and any subsequent product recalls are handled carefully as there could be serious consequences for the organisation. Some of the potential consequences are:

- Injury to customers/consumers – end users of the products may suffer from use of defective products, which could result in prosecution and claims for damages.

- Customer business performance – where manufacturers sell to retailers and the goods are then recalled, the retailer would suffer a loss of sales.

- Reputation – the manufacturer of a defective product would, almost certainly, have their reputation adversely affected by a product recall and the accompanying publicity. Where the manufacturer makes private-label goods for the retailer, the retailer will suffer the loss of reputation. It is then possible, even likely, that the retailer will terminate the supply contract, a loss of which might be big enough to force smaller suppliers out of business.

- Product liability legislation – the discovery of non-compliance and a subsequent product recall may draw the attention of public enforcement organisations such as Trading Standards, Health and Safety Executive (HSE) and the European Union (EU). This could lead to punitive fines and/or orders to close certain aspect of the business.

9.3.2   Case study

In 1999, Coca-Cola recalled 700,000 bottles of one of its products from the Belgian market after contamination by a sulphur compound. Products were also withdrawn from several markets around Europe, with French distribution chains reportedly withdrawing stocks of 50 million Coca-Cola products. Furthermore, the company's bottling plants in Dunkirk and Belgium were temporarily shut. The company reported that the product recall cost the group $60m.

9.3.3　Data management

The collection, recording and management of customer complaints data are key aspects of complaints management. Most companies have some way of recording complaints from customers. Opportunities are, however, lost when this recorded information is not converted into a form that would enable the company both to monitor its performance and to make lasting changes to its operations. There are a number of reasons why companies fail to maximise the opportunities, including:

- Resources – some companies, especially smaller ones, lack the human resources and time to analyse customer complaints data.

- Irrelevant information collection – if the wrong types of data are collected, then little or no useful information about customer complaints would be available to management.

- Company structure and culture – if the organisation has a culture that penalises non-conformance rather than seeking inclusive solutions, employees may suppress complaints information and, in particular, the more serious complaints. Furthermore, if the company structure does not designate responsibility for complaints management (customer service department, quality department, etc.), the management of complaints data may be patchy and incomprehensive at best.

- Management commitment – if the company's management adopts a fire-fighting attitude to customer complaints resolution, then it is unlikely that any data, if collected at all, will be used to develop robust solutions to the root causes of non-conformance.

Although the benefits from the recording and management of complaints data are important, the effort required should not be under-estimated. The company may not only have to collect 'front office' data such as number, type and medium of complaints, but also 'back office' data such as potential and actual liability cost, cause of complaint, resolution time, communication with customer and preventive action. Data may also be collected on factors such as staff costs and productivity changes resulting from complaints management.

9.4 Key Summary Points

- Most customers will not complain, so every complaint should be taken seriously as it has probably impacted on other customers
- Complaints that are quickly and satisfactorily resolved lead to even more loyal customers
- Always identify and deal with the root cause of the problem and not just the symptom
- Develop an 'emergency' or 'disaster' plan
- Keep customers informed at all stages of the complaint investigation and resolution

9.5 Further Reading

Gober M. (2000). Increasing your confidence with complaints. *Customer Management*, 28-9.

Hill N. (1999). Customer satisfaction measurement. *Customer Service Management*, 39-42.

Hutchins D. Managing a product recall. *Quality World*, 30-2.

Reichheld F.F. (1996). Learning from customer defections. *Harvard Business Review*, 56-69.

TMI & ICS. (2001). *National Complaints Culture Survey 2001*. TMI, UK (www.tmi.co.uk).

10. HOW TECHNOLOGY AND PEOPLE CAN IMPACT ON CUSTOMER SATISFACTION

10.1   Introduction

Companies are now increasingly aware of how the use of technology, especially the Internet, and having the right people working for the organisation can have an impact on how the company services and satisfies its customers. This chapter examines these issues with a view to seeking the hidden value that lies in these approaches to organisational management.

10.2   The Internet

Organisations, in general, structure a large part of their corporate strategy on two key issues – offering (what to sell) and service (how to sell). Traditionally, the dimensions for sales have been limited, depending on the company's business and the type of customers that it serves; for example, food retailers do not sell by telephone or mail order, and produce dealers selling on spot markets do not offer continuous replenishment facilities. The complexities and difficulties associated with selling identical products in different ways have often meant that companies have been completely unable to service certain sections of the market.

The advance of technology and the developments in the use of the Internet have opened up a wide range of opportunities to organisations in all sectors. Significantly, it has also brought new threats, particularly with respect to increased and transparent competition from previously unheard-of peers.

The basic rules remain the same – develop the appropriate strategy to attract and keep the right customers. To do this implies a marriage of both technology and strategy. It is not enough just to have a Web presence. Consequently, the organisation will need to make the right decisions from a wide variety of choices, ranging from its Web site's facilities to procurement over the Internet.

10.2.1   The Web site

A company's Web site is often the first contact that new and, in particular, distant customers have with the organisation and its products. Customers often want a site that is easy to navigate and that provides a reasonable amount of information without compromising on download times. It is a good idea to compare the company's Web site with other Web sites and to ask customers for their views on how the Web site can be improved. It is also important that the Web address is easy both to find and to remember – e.g. by using the company's name or product or service.

Web sites that are interactive are even more important if companies are serious about attracting and retaining customers. The ability to make enquiries online or even 'chat' in real time with a representative of the company implies that customers can get answers quickly and are then less likely to go to the competition, particularly if competing organisations do not have sites that provide a high level of service.

For organisations that deal with or wish to deal with a significant number of customers, there are both cost and marketing benefits to be gained from a good Web strategy – cross-selling on the Web site and via e-mail as well as a reduction of call-centre costs.

10.2.2   e-Market places

Business-to-business e-market places typically improve value for customers by providing information that enables decision making throughout the purchasing process. It is estimated that e-market places typically reduce customers' purchase cost by 20-25%. This places new pressures on sellers, particularly in commodity markets. A focus on cost reduction and buying from e-market places increases the likelihood that traditional customer-supplier relationships will be weakened since buying takes place on the spot market. However, for value-added, specialised or sensitive products, the likelihood is that customers will continue to forge relationships and partnerships with suppliers. McKinsey & Company and CAPS research have identified five types of B2B e-market places – project/specification managers, supply co-ordinators, liquidity creators, aggregators and transaction facilitators (see Further reading).

10.2.3 Clicks and mortar

The turbulence that has plagued the Internet and dot-com worlds has led to the recognition that the companies that would prosper in the new economy are those that can successfully manage the traditional physical business models together with the Internet business opportunities. This is commonly referred to as the clicks and mortar strategy.

The key issue to be addressed then becomes the extent to which the traditional business should be merged with the Internet business. The two key options that appear to face UK companies are:

- An integrated strategy where e-business is just another way of doing what the company already does – essentially an add-on to provide a new channel for sales or purchasing or operations management. An example of this is the online sales service of food retailers such as Tesco and Sainsbury's.

- A devolved strategy in which the traditional and Internet businesses are kept apart, with each having a different management and even different identities and branding. Examples of these can be found in the financial sector, where traditional businesses such as Halifax and the Co-operative Bank have set up separate online businesses – 'If' and 'Smile', respectively.

Both options have strengths and weaknesses, and the option to be selected by each company will depend on their current businesses and the vision of where they want to take their businesses. Some of the specific factors they will need to consider are discussed below.

10.2.3.1 Operations

The ability to merge operations depends to a great extent on the capabilities of the current system. Where there is good infrastructure or existing capacity in supply chain management, there is the ability to transfer these strengths to the online business with a considerable amount of cost saving. Having separate operations will mean new capital but will enable bespoke, targeted and modern systems. These options are primarily relevant where the company has integrated its traditional and Internet businesses. Where the two businesses are completely separate, it is unlikely that there will be any scope for the integration of operations.

10.2.3.2   Identity

Where Internet and traditional businesses are merged, a company with a strong brand recognition has the potential to leverage this strength while giving its customers new options – e.g. buy online and have goods delivered or collect at nearest store. This, however, limits the company in ways that will not be relevant if the traditional and Internet businesses have separate identities. For example, a merged identity may limit the ability to target new sets of customers or alter product range significantly. Internet banks, for example, have products and offers that differ from those of their parent companies and that are often targeted at particular groups in the society.

10.2.3.3   Marketing

Merging businesses provide an opportunity for cross-marketing of both goods and services, e.g. Internet-only or in-store promotions/events. On the other hand, if a company decides to have two separate identities for its businesses, then cross-marketing in itself becomes contradictory and may confuse customers.

10.2.3.4   Management structure

Having a separate management structure implies that both businesses can be more focused and innovative and develop different cultures. Typically, Internet businesses are perceived as less formal and 'savvy' in their approach. However, the ability to manage knowledge and benefit from legacy systems is reduced when both businesses have different management and focus. However, some backroom operations (e.g. purchasing, invoicing) could still be merged even when management in independent.

Whatever integration strategy a company adopts, what is clear is that modern technology can result in both operational and strategic benefits for the company. The key benefits include:

- Customer service – By understanding customer purchase patterns and preferences, a customised offering can be delivered. Furthermore, the ability to track customer purchase history implies that customers that reduce their patronage or are candidates for defection are more transparent and can then be approached to sort out any problems with meeting their specific needs. A Web presence also provides an opportunity for customers to complain when they are not happy with goods or services.

- Operations – Companies that deal with other businesses can benefit greatly by moving aspects of their operations online. Where a company links its systems with those of the customers, purchase intentions for the next period are easily available and can be fed back to other aspects of the business, e.g. production and distribution. In some cases, this can be linked further up the supply chain with the company's own supplies, thereby providing almost seamless alignment along the supply chain. In addition, invoicing, delivery scheduling and delivery tracking can all be carried out online. The net result is that there is great potential to improve customer service and satisfaction, reduce costs and improve efficiency.

However, companies also need to be aware of some of the difficulties that these new opportunities will bring. They might need to change their business philosophy and also need to ensure that their traditional business and their Internet business, whether integrated or not, are complementary and not in competition with each other.

10.2.4   Cost transparency and customer e-loyalty

The notions of cost transparency and customer loyalty on the Internet are, to a considerable extent, contradictory. There is no general consensus on whether the Internet can increase customer loyalty through 'stickiness' or reduce it through cost transparency. The experiences of companies differ significantly and, for the purposes of this book, we shall examine the underlying arguments for each case.

10.2.4.1   Cost transparency

The Internet has provided customers with a free, convenient and virtually limitless range of information about product attributes, costs, prices and competitors. This is true of both B2B and business-to-consumer (B2C) models.

With a few easy key strokes, a mid-size manufacturer can discover that a bag of sugar is 20% cheaper if bought from a supplier 30 or 40 miles away, while the young teenager soon discovers that his or her pocket money can buy more CDs if purchased from an online retailer. The key danger here is that, for the first time, customers can 'see through' supplier costs and determine whether the supplier is charging inconveniently high margins. This, of course, is counter to what most suppliers want and can lead not only to a reduction in customer loyalty but also to a perception of unfairness and profiteering by the supplier. Furthermore, the increasing popularity of on-line auctions and e-market places often means that individual companies or consortiums of companies can reduce their purchase cost by both buying at bulk prices and eliminating one or more layers of middle men.

In addition to cost transparency, the Internet can also provide information on service and performance transparency. It is now much easier for current and potential customers to compare attributes such as product functionality and lead times of a range of options from different parts of the world without leaving their desks or running up high costs.

To limit the negative effects of transparency, suppliers can consider the following:

- 'Shift' pricing, where prices are changed to reflect market conditions, local competition and costs of servicing individual customers (e.g. lead times, credit requests, geographical considerations).

- 'Layered' pricing, where different products are sold at different prices to meet the requirements of different customers. This is visible in the kinds of price structure that telecommunications and Internet service providers offer for their products.

- Optimising brand loyalty by the promise of reliability. This is one of the key arguments for e-loyalty and is discussed in greater detail later.

- Dominating a niche market by providing a product or service that cannot be easily matched and provides value to the customer.

- 'Obscuring' price transparency by bundling products and services; e.g. cable companies can now provide Internet access, telephone lines and cable television in one package. Similarly, utility companies can provide gas, electricity, telephone and even insurance in one package.

10.2.4.2   E-loyalty

In contrast to the notion of cost transparency and weakened customer loyalty, proponents of e-loyalty assert that Internet customers can be loyal in both B2B and B2C models. The contention is that the principles that hold true for traditional businesses are also relevant to Internet businesses – it costs more to recruit a new customer that to keep an old one and repeat purchases provide greatest value and build 'relationships'. From the experiences of companies that have achieved e-loyalty success, the following appear to be vital:

- Trust and brand – Customers want to deal with products that they can trust. This creates opportunities for organisations with strong brands. It is important to note that, while the Internet provides cost transparency, it does not guarantee quality, and low-priced items are not always good value. Suppliers can, however, extend their 'brand' to include service performance – so it is possible for customers to associate a supplier with on-time and in-full delivery every time. This sort of performance could then become a 'brand' of the company that delivers customer value and supports loyalty. To facilitate this, customers need to trust that the supplier's e-business system allows for accurate understanding of their requirements, backroom operations are efficiently linked with customer interface operations, electronic invoicing would be free of errors, etc.

- Customer selection – Attracting good value customers is important to e-loyalty. Traditional marketing initiatives were often focused on certain types of customer. The Internet, however, offers the opportunity to reach a much wider range of potential customers and it appears reasonable for a company to want to attract as many customers as possible. It is, however, almost impossible for a Web site to be everything to everybody – attempting this would lead to complexity and compromise of the e-customer experience in terms of available information, download time, ease of navigating, etc. The key learning is to use the Web to attract more of the type of customer that the company wants rather than try to attract all types of customer. Customers are attracted by various factors in e-business (price, brand, convenience, responsiveness, range, etc.) and it is important to take these into account when developing an e-business strategy.

- Marketing differentiation – By understanding customers' buying patterns and product and service preferences, e-marketing allows for pro-active and focused contact with customers to offer new products or services that would be of value to them or to inform of improvements or expected improvement to current product and service offerings.

10.3   Six Sigma Methodologies

The Six Sigma concept was popularised by Motorola. At the heart of this set of quality tools and techniques is the aim of achieving a maximum of 3.4 defects for every million units of service and product. In addition to the reduction in defect rates, the adoption of the concept also brings significant benefits, particularly in terms of cost savings, increased efficiency and improvement-oriented cultural change. Furthermore, the reduction of defect rates has been known to be instrumental in increasing customer satisfaction.

In developing the concept, Motorola defined a defect as anything that led to a degree of customer dissatisfaction. This definition implies that, although Six Sigma is a technical subject, it is very much focused on the customer. It is also a versatile tool that can be applied to many aspects of a company's operation, ranging from the actual product to appropriate time utilisation. It has even been used to improve efficiency in processing court cases in Bedfordshire Magistrates' Court.

From the above discussion, it is reasonable to concur that Six Sigma is based on the following underlying principles:

- reduction of variation in units of product or service
- reduction of the cost of non-conformance
- optimisation of resource utilisation

Typically, Six Sigma projects tend to have aggressive goals, which are often cost-related. The adoption of Six Sigma can also play an important role in marketing as it increases customer confidence in the ability of the company to both monitor and improve product and service quality. Furthermore, the successful implementation of the concept will put the company in a position to guarantee its customers a pre-defined level of quality.

However, the start-up costs of Six Sigma are not insignificant. Substantial amounts will need to be spent on training and software. Furthermore, members of the project team will have to take time off their day-to-day duties to participate in the programme. Larger organisations have been known to have full-time Six Sigma teams. Six Sigma also requires the company to develop a tendency for continuous improvement. While many projects will deliver quick wins, the company, as a whole, must keep striving to get better in all aspects of its operation.

10.4   People

In the year 2000, Xerox launched a company-wide programme called 'Customer First'. The aim of the programme was to ensure that all of its 92,000 employees appreciated and understood that they were all responsible for and had a role to play in satisfying the customer. This new sort of thinking is based on the increasing awareness that customer satisfaction is not based just on the quality of a company's products but on the total experience that a customer has when dealing with the company. This is even more important in the service industry, where there is more contact with a wider range of customers with even more diverse requirements. Companies such as Sears have recognised that the way in which their employees impact on the customers has a direct link with the profitability of the business.

As with most initiatives, the responsibility for creating people-customer satisfaction must start from the top. The senior management of the company needs to continually impress on the other employees that the satisfaction of the customer must be a key feature of all aspects of the company's operations. To achieve this, however, they must empower their staff and eliminate obstacles that stand between their employees and the customer.

The following examples give an idea of the principles and methods adopted by two leading companies whose business models bring them into contact with millions of customers every year. It is important to appreciate that the underlying principles are equally applicable to manufacturing businesses.

10.4.1   Wal-Mart

Wal-Mart is an American company with operations all over the world. As a leading retailer, it is well known for low prices, a wide product range and product quality. Wal-Mart recognises that, through the provision of exceptional service and commitment to customers, its employees contribute vitally to its success. To facilitate this, the Company:

- believes in its people and looks after them by providing a wide range of benefits for both full-time and part-time staff. The possession of 'people skills' is also a key consideration in the employment process.

- communicates extensively and openly with all employees. The Company stresses the fact that all are working towards a common goal and encourages feedback and ideas for improvement from all its staff. Communication is achieved in a variety of ways, including the well-recognised daily customer service meetings, through weekly international TV broadcasts, to magazines and regular executive meetings.

- trains its employees extensively through the development of different training programmes that best suit individual employees.

- rewards and recognises employees who exceed expectations. Recognition is primarily a public affair, with reward taking forms that range from promotions to bonuses.

The success of Wal-Mart with respect to people development is also evident in its UK operations at Asda Supermarkets. In 2002, Asda was rated first in *The Times* list of the best UK companies to work for.

10.4.2   The Hard Rock Café (HRC)

HRC is an organisation that has achieved a strong international brand image and recognition. It is a high-end business that is usually associated with the glamour of movie and music stars. Behind the glitz and glamour lies a strong sense of community among its staff. Employees are treated with respect and sufficiently resourced and empowered to carry out their functions.

The organisation provides benefits that supersede those offered by most of its peers and actively promotes retention of employees through recognition, rewards and job reassignments to all parts of the world.

To promote its people focus, the Company has developed a fashionable staff handbook that educates, in a fun way, how to treat customers. In addition, a bill of rights for its employees has been developed.

10.5 'People' Approaches

Customer-successful organisations understand the important role played by committed staff in meeting their objectives. Staff commitment is more often than not a result of deliberate policies and practices aimed at both making employees enjoy their work and satisfy customers at the same time. There are a number of approaches that can be applied to improve the people-customer-profit link. These include:

- Leadership – the emphasis is on leaders having personal involvement through encouraging staff, mentoring and being role models. This would involve promoting two-way communication within the organisation.

- Training – the emphasis is on training people in the skills and use of technology that would facilitate the provision of service to customers.

- Teamwork – employees are encouraged to work in teams and to provide support for each other with the primary goal being to improve the customer experience. The feeling of belonging and camaraderie is commonly viewed as a key reason why employees enjoy their work. In a teamwork environment, employees also strive to ensure that they do not let down the rest of the team.

- Empowerment – front-line staff are empowered to make certain types of decisions on behalf of the company without reference to managers and supervisors. This gives the employees a sense of responsibility while dealing with customer issues at the first point of contact. Very often, the financial and goodwill cost of re-directing customers to the 'right' person or department is more that the cost if it had been resolved at the first point of contact (see case study D on Northern Ireland Electricity).

- Reward and recognition – reward and recognition systems are increasingly including service provided to customers as a key consideration. In some instances, (e.g. hotels) customers are encouraged to nominate a member of staff that has provided outstanding service.

The approach(es) to be adopted by each organisation will be dependent on factors such as the culture within the organisation, the customer, services provided and organisational values (see case study E on an IT company).

10.6 Key Summary Points

- Technology impacts on the way customers buy and manufacturers produce and sell; use it for your organisation's benefits
- The Internet has enabled greater cost transparency
- No customer development effort will be successful if the people that work for the organisation do not believe in it and 'work' for the customer as well
- Develop, train, encourage and recognise employees that impact positively on the customer

10.7 Further Reading

Anderson D. (2000). The secret behind that Wal-Mart smile. *Customer Management*, 12-13.

Anon. (2000). Does your customer service rock'n'roll. *Customer Management*, 6-11.

Armistead C., Beamish N., Kiely J. (2001). *Emerging Skills for a Changing Economy*. Institute of Customer Service, UK.

McKinsey & Co. and CAPS Research. (2000). Coming into focus – using the lens of economic value to clarify the impact of B2B e-marketplaces. www.mckinsey.com or www.capsresearch.org.

PART 2: CASE STUDIES IN CUSTOMER SATISFACTION

11. CASE STUDY A: PERNOD RICARD

11.1   Background

Pernod Ricard was created more than 25 years ago. Until the year 2000, the Company was primarily a spirits company. With the acquisition of Seagram's spirit and wine business (in partnership with Diageo) in that year, the Company became one of the three largest spirits and wine companies in the world, with its turnover for that year increasing by 22%. The Company owns some of the biggest and most recognised spirits and wine brands worldwide, including Chivas Regal, Jameson, Martell, Dubonnet, Cinzano and Jacob's Creek.

Pernod Ricard UK has built a successful business in the UK. This has been facilitated by a strong focus on customer satisfaction. As a measure of the importance of customer satisfaction to the business, the customer service department (CSD) has grown from 3 people to 11 people within the past 3 years and has a reputation of the most envied department in the company. The Company has developed a 5-year (2001-2006) customer satisfaction strategy with clearly identifiable targets.

Success has, however, not come without the commitment and creativity of the CSD and a few challenges along the way.

11.2   The Customer Service Department (CSD)

The acquisition of Seagram's brands in 2000 resulted in an expansion of the CSD. Although both companies had previously dealt primarily with the same organisations (i.e. customers, distributors, etc.) their customer service functions had, understandably, worked in different ways. In order to manage this combination of cultures, the department evolved organically. A key change was the move away from an individual-based structure to a team-based structure, which was developed through brainstorming sessions and focus groups. All team members were involved and empowered to write their own team roles and job descriptions. Responsibility is equally shared and all members of the department are encouraged to voice their opinions.

Every year, the department holds a 'customer service week', which affords the opportunity for social activities. It is also commonplace to recognise and celebrate the birthdays of members of the team.

The department owes it success, among other factors, to the involvement, empowerment and creativity of its people. The Company does not operate a call centre facility and this helps the CSD to develop better relationships with the customers. All customer service executives (CSEs) are empowered to take necessary steps to deal with customer issues without having to seek approval through a chain of command. The department also has a 'buddy' system and CSEs tend to specialise in a particular sector, although job rotation is encouraged and has been taken up in the past.

In total, the team deal with about 700 customers, although most trade is done with national customers such as the big supermarket chains.

11.3   Customer Perception Survey

A key driver of the success of the CSD is the customer perception survey. This has been carried out since 1999 but was adjusted to include the new businesses acquired in 2000. To provide objectivity and professionalism, the survey is carried out by the Customer Service Network, an independent organisation. The 5-year customer strategy is based on results of the surveys. The Company also uses the surveys as a tool to benchmark the Company's performance against that of competitors.

The survey itself comprises both quantitative and qualitative questions. A summary of the 2001 surveys showed overall customer satisfaction of 89.4% with 47.1% of respondents claiming to have noticed an improvement in services in the previous 12 months.

As a matter of routine, the results of the survey are sent to customers with a pledge of improvement actions to be taken. Many of the initiatives presented in this case study are based on survey results.

11.4   Third Party Partnership

Customer perception surveys indicated that delivery was a key area for improvement. This indicated the need to work closely with the Company's third party delivery organisation. The Company views the organisation as a partner and, as a result of the push to improve, the delivery organisation has developed new practices, which it has also applied to other customers.

There is an agreed 98% service level agreement between both organisations, which is measured quarterly. When performance falls below this target, the delivery company pays compensation of £4,000, but, when performance is above the target, Pernod Ricard pays recognition of the same sum of money.

All delivery queries are logged by Pernod Ricard and a daily operations report is developed and copies sent to the delivery company to ensure that all indicated problems are dealt with effectively and promptly.

Both companies have formed a joint steering group to improve the overall delivery performance and help implement agreed actions.

As part of their induction process, all Pernod Ricard CSEs spend a day on the road with the drivers of the delivery company in order to get an experience of the frustrations faced. This also helps build relationships with drivers who 'represent' Pernod Ricard to customers even though they work for a totally different company. On a less formal level, employees from the delivery company are invited to participate in social and promotional events arranged by Pernod Ricard.

11.5   Customer Relationships

Pernod Ricard UK has developed visions and values to support its business. These were developed entirely by the workforce with the encouragement of management. The values are Energy, Working together, Communication, Care, Excellence, Profit-minded. The work of the CSD and the way it relates to customers strongly reflect these corporate values. The CSD aims to deliver the 'perfect transaction' to all customers. Initiatives that have been developed include the following.

- A 'sorry' card – a postcard-size card is sent to customers when there has been a problem. The card acknowledges the problem and details improvement actions that the Company has taken. This initiative, which was developed in 2000, has been well received by customers.

- Whenever a customer has been sent a 'sorry' card, the account is flagged as a priority account and extra special care is taken to ensure that no further problems occur with the customer.

- The CSD encourages its customers to complain when things go wrong. The philosophy practised by the department is that, when things sometimes go wrong, it is a great chance to improve and to build relationships.

- The CSEs get to know their customers and build relationships with them. This in many cases makes customers become more like friends. For example, when a customer was in hospital, the company sent get-well cards and gifts.

- The CSD is currently developing a 'pledge' card, which will inform customers of what to expect from the Company. This will be included in the 'Welcome' pack for new customers.

- The CSD also identifies customers with declining transactions and uses this information to find out if there has been a service or product problem.

- A freephone number to encourage customer communication has been made operational.

- CSEs are also given the flexibility to identify customer needs as part of routine operations in addition to the annual survey.

- As part of the drive for the perfect transaction, all customer orders are confirmed before delivery to the person who made the order (in addition to the person to receive the stock). On the night before scheduled delivery, the schedule is confirmed with the delivery company and the warehouse. In the morning, the CSD confirms that the delivery vehicle has been loaded and is on the way. The customer is then called to re-confirm the delivery and give an estimate of the expected delivery time. Any problems are immediately relayed to the customer and alternative arrangements made.

- The CSD has developed the 'just 5 minutes' mini survey, which is sent out on a quarterly basis to a cross-section of customers. The anonymous mini-survey focuses on just one aspect of operations (e.g. delivery) and is designed to give a quick snapshot of operational effectiveness.

- The CSD has extended its office hours to facilitate more convenience for the customers.

11.6   Mystery Shopping

The customer service department initiated mystery shopping within Pernod Ricard. This initiative was initially resisted by some people within the department but was later embraced when the benefits became obvious. Mystery shopping has been so successful within the department that it is now being used by other departments within the company.

This technique, which is more popular with consumer-facing organisations, is managed by the Customer Service Network, an independent organisation. A call is made to the CSD under the pretence of being a potential customer and the way in which the enquiry is handled in evaluated. Based on the evaluation, individual and departmental quarterly updates on improvement are given. There is always room for improvement as the questions asked become more sophisticated and the expectations become higher.

11.7   Personnel Development

To enable the success it has achieved with customer satisfaction, Pernod Ricard has invested in its people. Individual training needs are identified through an annual appraisal system. A budget for training is sought from senior management. CSEs have been trained in telephone skills and how to respond to customer complaints. As a result of comments from the customer survey, CSEs have been sent on in-house courses to give them more knowledge about the Company's brands. Currently, customer service NVQ3 is being introduced into the department.

11.8   Summary

The CSD at Pernod Ricard has successfully faced the dual challenge of merging cultures with rapid business growth. This success has largely been due to the efforts made to know and understand their customers and to understand their own organisation. Perhaps more importantly, there is a culture of continuous improvement and the CSD has been proactive in dealing with customer-related challenges.

12. CASE STUDY B:
BRITISH TELECOMMUNICATIONS PLC

The author, Steve Keen, joined BT in 1980, after 3 years teaching English. Beginning in Customer Service roles, he then moved into Marketing before taking his current post in Group Strategy.

12.1   Company Background

Ten years ago, BT employed 200,000 people, had a turnover of £11.1bn and made profits of £2.8bn. Within the telecommunications services market in the UK, there was only one other company, Mercury Communications Limited (MCL).

In the year to April 1999, BT employees numbered 125,000, turnover was £18.2bn and operating profit £3.5bn. The Company was facing over 200 competitors, and MCL had become a part of Cable & Wireless Communications, which has itself become subject to a takeover by NTL, a company that barely even existed 5 years ago.

With the increased number of competitors, and with the accompanying increase in the number of services available, customer awareness of the many alternatives has risen, and with that raised awareness has come raised expectations of what service providers are able to do for them.

12.2   Customer Satisfaction

Customer satisfaction can be defined as "The extent to which a company is able to meet or exceed its customers' expectations". David Maister (The Psychology of Waiting Lines, 1988) has expressed this as a formula (Maister's First Law of Service):

$$Satisfaction = Perception - Expectation$$

Customer perception is vital, because to paraphrase Tom Peters: it doesn't matter how good you are; what matters is how good your customers think you are. BT has literally thousands of internal measures showing how we are performing operationally. Whilst these are indispensable as real measures of performance, they can also be misleading if they are not compared with customer feedback.

The company therefore talks to its customers through a number of Market Research programmes in order to identify customer satisfaction drivers, using a variety of methodologies, both qualitative and quantitative, *ad hoc* and continuous.

One of the outputs of this research is a satisfaction model (Fig. 12.1), which identifies and weighs elements of service from a customer's perspective.

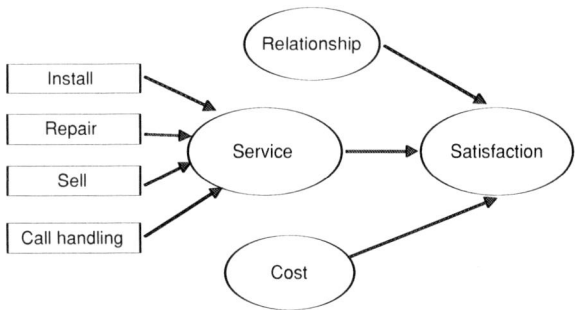

Fig. 12.1. BT business customer satisfaction model (summarised)

In the full model, each of the lines has a value assigned that represents the relative contribution the upstream attribute makes to that immediately downstream. The model is based upon a monthly satisfaction survey; values are determined through regression analysis.

Using this and other models and analyses we are able to determine that, whilst there is a positive link between customer satisfaction and customer loyalty, there is no such thing as a 100% guarantee in this link. Furthermore, if operational performance remains static, satisfaction does not, as rising expectations of service act as a gravitational pull on satisfaction levels. The Company is also aware that there are some elements of service that are essential to customers, but which are not in themselves drivers of satisfaction because it is taken for granted that these things will happen, such as obtaining dial tone, or service delivery at an agreed time. These are the "Hygiene Factors" shown in the hierarchy below (Fig. 12.2).

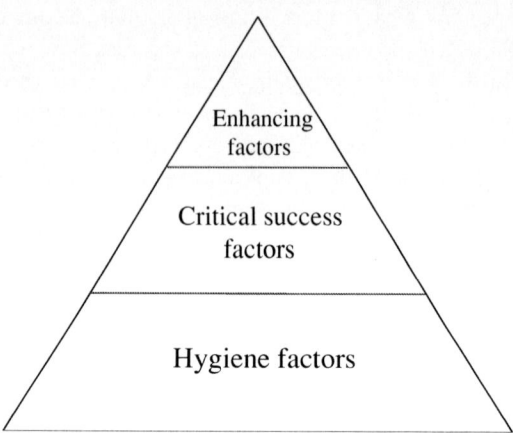

Fig. 12.2. Drivers of satisfaction hierarchy

It is only once Critical Success Factors (CSFs) are present that Customer Satisfaction is achieved. These may include such things as good account management or the ability to meet a very short timescale. Given the drag of expectation, however, many CSFs are destined to become Hygiene Factors.

Further, it is only once we are able to achieve the Enhancing Factors that true Loyalty and Commitment are built. These will include the ability truly to enter into a partnership with the customer, understanding the customer's needs and wants, and displaying that almost telepathic quality demonstrated by the best salespeople of knowing that the customer needs something even before the customer knows it.

The corollary of this is that the absence of Enhancing Factors excludes the possibility of any long-term customers; failure to achieve CSFs results in commoditisation, the concentration on charging the lowest price for an undifferentiated product; and failure to achieve even the Hygiene Factors will eventually end with the complete erosion of your customer base.

12.3   Determining the Key Satisfaction Measures

To be "effective" means "to do the right things". The ability to drive 100 miles from Central London in as many minutes may be efficient, but if you're on the

M1, heading north, and your destination is Bristol, to the west, you are hardly being effective.

Similarly, if I achieve optimum levels of Customer Satisfaction but fail to make a profit, my measurement programme is not effective to the business.

In monitoring satisfaction I need to understand the implications for Marketing and Customer Service:

- How do individual experiences impact?
- How can we implement uniform incremental improvements?
- How does the customer experience add up?
- How do we implement step changes?
- How do we get the message over?

The BT Satisfaction Model is marketing-oriented, looking at the long term and the big picture. It is supplemented by operational and tactical surveys, which are oriented to day-to-day service, event-driven and giving a more granular view, concentrating on the minutiae of the customer experience. Both types of research are continuously refreshed to provide an ongoing picture of satisfaction trends.

But, although they give an essential view of performance, the view they offer is like driving by the rear-view mirror. Neither, on its own, is able to provide a forward-looking view of the impact on customer satisfaction, and consequent financial return, of introducing changes to the service offering.

To do this BT has developed a Competitive Positioning Model (CPM).

The building blocks for CPM allow us to

- Identify drivers of positive loyalty to BT based on disposition and value
- Balance service quality, relationship and value
- Identify benchmarks for customer expectations
  - Other telecoms companies
  - 'Quality' competitors
  - External drivers of expectations – for example, computer and office equipment suppliers
- Prioritise actions to improve perceptions and values
- Segment customers based on value needs
- Package service to match value needs

But most critically, CPM enables us to forecast the revenue and profit impact of any actions we take, allowing us to run what-ifs on service and output a detailed revenue scenario.

The starting point in developing the CPM model was detailed qualitative research to provide an insight into the key drivers of customer loyalty and buying behaviour. This comprised:

- Focus groups and seminar days with customers across BT segments
- Paired depth interviews with key telecoms decision makers and influencers
- Telephone depth interviews focused on specific customer experience events

This represented one of the largest qualitative research projects ever undertaken by BT and spanned the customer base from global businesses to consumer.

The research provides inputs into:

- Developing a blueprint for service
- Understanding loyalty drivers
- Understanding the drivers of price perceptions and value
- Providing a framework for customer value analysis
- Segmenting customers in terms of value of service
- Identifying benchmarks that drive expectations
- Exploring switching triggers and dynamics

Following on from this stage, wide-ranging quantitative research has been carried out to quantify priority actions and to feed into the final model.

A schematic framework for the model is shown below (Fig. 12.3), identifying each of the key components used in revenue projection.

As illustrated, the model takes account of value of service, brand value and price, to predict brand preference based on detailed trade-off research. Service in this context covers the core product, customer service, technical expertise, sales and account management. Careful consideration is given to the softer elements of service, which are found to be as important as the core product attributes in driving supplier preference, and therefore essential in the brand preference model

In order to translate predicted brand preference into market share, the model also takes account of inertia, competitor reach – awareness and viability of competitors (both geographic and product), and market dynamics.

The inertia component is based on attitudinal segmentation covering the perceived risk, effort and upheaval in switching suppliers.

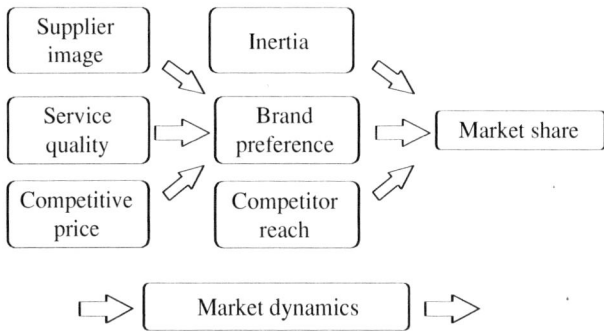

Fig. 12.3. Competitive Positioning Model

The competitor viability inputs are based on market intelligence using inputs from the BT competitive analysis team. Competitive analysis is also used to feed the model with up-to-date information on competitor pricing.

Finally, the market dynamics element takes account of the churn rates and triggers to competitor migration such as new growth, contract renewals, office moves and competitor activity.

The Competitive Positioning Model provides key inputs into a number of areas:

- Price positioning
- Value of service
- Brand value
- Market share projection

Specific applications of the model include:

- Setting service standards and targets
- Price positioning of products
- Rebalancing of prices
- Developing tariff and discount structures
- Supporting major business cases
- Design of optimal service and price package
- Target marketing segmentation
- Estimating the impact of campaigns to promote BT value

For example, a recent business case was tested for a major investment to bring about improvements to customer interface and account management. The model was able to estimate the impact this would have on improved customer retention and customer re-engagement potential.

Where the research has identified a number of such priorities it is possible to rank these in terms of their potential payback in relation to development costs.

In addition to scenario testing, as described above, standard outputs are used to pinpoint priorities based on:

- importance in driving loyalty
- performance in relation to competition (based on best in class)
- performance in relation to expectations

These can be modelled to highlight where actions are needed.

Specific action plans can then be developed and tested in the model to derive revenue impacts, which can be evaluated against implementation costs.

This type of revenue modelling can be used to produce cost/benefit analyses for business cases and by combining the models, ongoing prioritisation is possible, as shown below (Fig. 12.4).

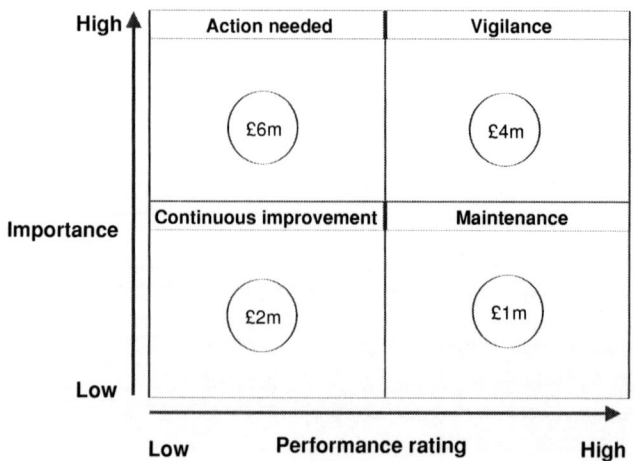

Fig. 12.4. Prioritising using performance, importance and projected revenue figures

It is in this way, taking into account the position of a specific service attribute on the Performance Importance Grid, coupled with a forecast of potential revenues from effecting an improvement in the attribute, that customer satisfaction measurement becomes truly effective.

12.4   Conclusion – An Accelerating World

To maintain position in your market, it is essential to ensure that a programme of continuous improvement is in place in your service organisation. As Maister says (Maister's Second Law of Service):

> "It's hard to play catch-up"

Continuous improvement needs to be complemented by a monitoring system that identifies the elements of service that deliver most value to both the customer and the business.

Since the introduction of telecommunications liberalisation, BT has undergone many changes in the way it delivers customer service, and the rate of change is constantly accelerating. The task confronting us can be summed up in the following extract from *Alice through the Looking Glass*:

> "Here, you see, it takes all the running you can do to keep in the same place," said the Queen. "If you want to get somewhere else, you must run at least twice as fast as that."

12.5   Acknowledgements

Bernard Chudy of Enteleca, for helping with the explanation of the Competitive Positioning Model, and Kate Roberts at Business & Market Research for the Drivers of Satisfaction Hierarchy.

This article first appeared in the International Journal of Customer Relationship Management.

13. CASE STUDY C: MAGRO BROTHERS (FOODS) LTD

13.1 Company Background

The Magro Brothers Group of Companies was founded in 1916 by three Magro brothers. They were traders in local agricultural produce, importers and distributors in livestock, fodder and general groceries and exporters of cotton and Maltese lace. In 1934, they ventured into the production of tomato paste from locally grown tomatoes for export to the British Commonwealth countries. In 1977, John and Michael Magro, the sons of one of the first partners, took over the running of the business and further expanded its activities to include tinplate can manufacture, foods distribution, retailing, advertising and marketing, and construction and real estate.

Today, Magro Brothers Group has become one of the leading enterprises in Malta and has gained the respect of the local business community and the trust of financial and commercial organisations. The Company is an active member of four Chambers of Commerce and, in 1998, it was bestowed with the prestigious award for Achievement in Industry. Furthermore, in 2000, it was chosen as the 'Most Consistent Export Performer' for the Maltese industry.

The key business of the food division of Magro Brothers Group is the processing of fresh tomatoes, with special emphasis on tomato ketchup for the export market. However, the product range also includes canned pulses, stock cubes and bouillons, mayonnaise, jams, pickled products and canned fruit.

13.2 Strategic Vision

Although the Company has been in the food export business since 1955, when it exported tomato paste in aluminium tubes to Britain, its main market continued to be the Maltese for a long time. In the early nineties, the Company decided to take a closer look at the export market and shortly afterwards a strategic decision was taken to increase focus on exports.

To facilitate this, the Company invested heavily in equipment and facilities and, in 1995, moved to a purpose-built factory with a covered area of 27,000 square metres and state-of-the-art manufacturing facilities. Today, the Company has one of the largest and most technologically advanced factories in the Mediterranean.

The Company now exports to more than 20 countries on a regular basis and has built up significant brand recognition in Malta and some other countries. The growth statistics are impressive – from a company that manufactured mainly for the local market, more than 40% of current production is for exports. This was made possible by managing to double its export figures year after year for the past 5 years. During the same period the Company also succeeded in increasing its share of the local market.

Of special interest is the UK market, which can be notoriously difficult to penetrate for new entrants. Magro Brothers started exports of its products to the UK in 1998 and today, 60% of its exports are sent to the UK. The list of clients is also very impressive, and includes two supermarket chains (including one of the 'big five') and one of the most recognisable fast food chains in the world.

Clearly, the increase in production capacity has been a key contributor to the Company's success, but the prime driver was and continues to be the Company's ability to offer exceptional service and value to its customers.

13.3   Customer Satisfaction Development

Magro Brothers' approach to dealing with customers is founded on a number of core principles supported by well developed processes and activities. The key factors are:

- Persistence and listening
- Bespoke services (value)
- True partnerships
- Communication
- Quality

13.3.1   Persistence and listening

Following the investment in plant and building and the decision to focus on the UK market, the Company was faced with the difficulty of breaking into the market. It took more than a year of phone calls and letters to be able to arrange the first ever meeting with a prospective UK customer, and the meeting did not get the best of starts. John Magro recalls that one of the first statements the buyer said was: 'I came to Gozo once and I hated it; I hated the wine, it was vinegar wine'. However, armed with his samples, John Magro was finally able to convince the prospective customer that world-class ketchup was produced in Malta. This persistence paid off and the discussions then focused on what value Magro Brothers could offer to the customer.

Listening to customers is closely tied in with listening to their needs. The relationship with the second major UK customer was based on both persistence and the ability to listen. The customer had been let down by another supplier and persistence meant that Magro Brothers was able to step in at short notice. However, this involved understanding that particular customer and its needs. The Company is always talking to and listening to its customers and prospective customers and, whenever an opportunity arises, the Company is flexible and nimble enough to satisfy.

13.3.2   Bespoke services (value)

One of the key strengths of the organisation is its ability to provide unique services to its customers. While most companies in the same market offer customers a narrow or pre-defined range of products and services, Magro Brothers' approach to the customer is 'Tell us what you want to make'. This approach has seen the Company develop the ability to supply products in a range of formats, including metal cans, glass bottles and jars, plastic containers and aluminium tubes. Furthermore, in the past, the Company has been able to fulfil non-standard requests such as unusual package sizes and numbers.

In addition, the Company has been able to develop a unique product for one of its key customers. This is discussed in some detail in the partnership sub-section.

13.3.3   True partnerships

In discussing his views about partnerships, Mr Magro said: 'I believe in relationships; I recognise that my client is my business partner.' This is a philosophy that has been put to positive use by the Company.

The Company has identified that its customers are interested not only in a product but also in the services that come with the product. For example, the fast food chain takes into account how its suppliers would react in a crisis and, to do this, both the supplier and the customer need to understand each other's businesses.

One of Magro Brothers' biggest partnership success has been in new product development. A few months after starting to supply one of the UK supermarket chains, Magro Brothers identified a gap in its client's product range. They then proposed a number of new product ideas to the customer. The customer liked one of the ideas and then a joint team from both Magro Brothers and the client company developed different recipes and specifications (e.g. texture, colour) that were relevant to the product's target market. Magro Brothers produced samples, which the client test marketed. The results were positive and full production commenced after teams from both companies had developed and agreed on the product label and the packaging type.

Consequently, by understanding its customer's business, Magro Brothers was able to propose a win-win idea that was developed successfully through partnership. This win-win approach to partnerships is also used on the rare occasions when there are service difficulties. When both companies were let down by a third party, a meeting was held at board level and the issues were jointly resolved by the customer suggesting a more reliable UK logistics company to Magro Brothers. Thus the customer used its local knowledge to help Magro Brothers provide it with better service.

Equally importantly, Magro Brothers has partnerships with all its key suppliers. All are met regularly and the Company develops multiple communication channels at all levels of its suppliers' organisation. This has been very instrumental in the meeting of special needs; for example, when the Company needed to supply a new customer at short notice, partnerships with label suppliers meant that a whole new range of labels could be produced and developed within a lead time that would have been impossible if partnerships had not been established.

13.3.4   Communication

The ability to communicate effectively is the most critical aspect of Magro Brothers' approach to customer satisfaction. Developing partnerships, delivering value and producing quality would all be difficult if there was no proper communication in the first place. For a company whose operational base is located more than a thousand miles away from its customers, Magro Brothers does better at communicating than local companies, in our opinion.

While all the modern communication techniques (telephone, Internet, fax, etc.) are available for use, Magro Brothers has gone a step further. The Company has employed a UK-based agent whose sole responsibility is to provide support to the current customers. The agent visits each of Magro Brothers' key UK customers every week to make sure that there are no problems with the product or service provided by the Company. Furthermore, the agent's visits are not confined to customers' head offices, but include operational bases such as depots and stores.

This approach means that any problems are uncovered in a matter of days and quickly resolved, in some cases, through partnership with the customer. Perhaps more importantly, this approach assures the customer that the Company cares and that any issues that arise will be dealt with speedily. It is also noteworthy that the UK-based agent is not required to look for new customers for the Company but only to make sure that current customers are satisfied with Magro Brothers' service.

The lines of communication between the UK agent and the company base in Gozo are also well established. One of the managers in Gozo has overall responsibility for identifying and correcting the root cause of any potential problems and, as such, is in touch with the UK agent at least once a week.

13.3.5   Quality

In line with much of current thinking, Magro Brothers believes and accepts that product quality is now a standard feature in the food industry. If it cannot meet and exceed expectations on product specification, there would be no business in the first place. To ensure that it produces goods of premium quality, the Company sources its local raw materials from farmers and other partners with whom relationships have been established for years. These suppliers are aware of the specific needs of Magro Brothers (quality, quantity, storage conditions, delivery schedules, etc.). All tomatoes are electronically scanned for quality. This ensures that only the best-quality raw materials go into the final product. The Company's philosophy is 'Quality is the customer coming back and not the product'. With respect to its processes, the Company complies with ISO 9002 standards and is regularly assessed against British Retail Consortium (BRC) technical standards.

The approach to quality goes beyond the product and also focuses on the people that work for the Company. Mr Magro believes that quality is a culture and everybody must breathe it. To facilitate this, the Company has recently brought in a psychologist to examine the motivation of everyone within the Company. This has met with a positive response from the workforce.

13.4   Future Plans

The Company plans to build on its past successes. In particular, it will remain flexible and continue to offer value to both existing and potential customers. The successes gained with respect to partnerships will also be re-visited and the Company has identified a new range of premium specialist products that are currently missing from its customers' ranges. It is expected that these opportunities will be further profitably developed in partnership with customers. To sum up, Mr Magro said: 'We are always looking to talk to people and develop partnerships; when you have a partnership, things go smoothly, when you don't, things fail'.

14. CASE STUDY D: NORTHERN IRELAND ELECTRICITY

14.1   Background

Northern Ireland Electricity (NIE) is a Belfast-based subsidiary of Viridian Group plc. The Company employs 1,200 people and serves 688,000 customers in Northern Ireland. In 2000, NIE transmitted more than 7,000 Gigawatt hours (Gwh) of electricity through a network of 66,500 transformers and related sub-stations over a distance of 35,000 miles.

The first 5 years of NIE's existence as a private sector company were characterised by a focus of building a good track record of customer satisfaction, among other attributes. This focus has been supported by NIE's quality journey, which started in 1993 and led to the adoption and company-wide implementation of the EFQM Excellence Model. The Company's success is evidenced by its winning the UK Excellence Awards in 2001 and the Northern Ireland Millennium Quality Award for Business Excellence. In addition, the Company's Customer Service business staff achieved the prestigious Charter Mark for Excellence in Customer Service as far back as 1997.

14.2   Approach

The Company has a mission to:

> "Provide excellence in customer service by delivering products and services that are recognised by our customers as being exceptionally efficient and value-for-money."

This mission statement is supported by the identification of 'customer focus' as one of the key values of the organisation. Customer focus is defined as 'meeting our external and internal customers' expectations in terms of quality, competitiveness and service delivery.'

The strategy used to achieve NIE's customer satisfaction objectives consists of a number of integrated processes and activities, which include customer contact, customer information and customer organisation.

14.2.1 Customer contact

Customer contact is encouraged and supported throughout the whole organisation. Employees at all levels and in various functions meet with customers on a regular basis and, furthermore, the Company has differentiated its different types of customers and uses the most appropriate type for contact for the relevant customers. The ways in which customers are contacted include:

- NIE's senior managers meet with the top 50 customers personally, each year. This is done either through business-to-business contacts or through formal visits to customer premises. This is carried out for business customers rather than residential customers.

- Customer Service Centre managers spend at least 70% of their time with consumer groups, business groups, local councillors, special needs community groups, charities, etc., in order to gauge customer opinion and understand requirements.

- Consumer Councils (such as the Northern Ireland Consumer Committee for Electricity) are also used as important sounding boards of customer opinion. Key managers from NIE have monthly one-to-one sessions with such councils.

- NIE conducts extensive market research and uses professionally recognised and independent research consultants in order to ensure non-bias and confidentiality to those taking part. Surveys are carried out for both domestic and commercial customers.

- NIE has an expanded emergency call-handling capability that makes it easier for customers to make the vital initial contact in times of difficulty.

- NIE has also set up a dedicated customer contact team to reduce the number of 'hand-overs' when customers phone the Company. The team is made up of specialists who will deal with a customer query or complaint first-hand and will transfer a call only if it needs the input of an expert. Where calls are transferred, they are transferred to a specific individual rather than a department.

- NIE has also introduced customer relationship managers whose job is to understand local issues in greater detail and feed the information back to the customer services teams. They also sort out local customer needs quickly.

14.2.2 Customer information

To ensure that its ability to make contact with the customers makes a positive impact on its business, the Company has developed processes that enable two-way flow of information. Perhaps more importantly, the Company ensures that the information that it processes is relevant to the needs of the customers and helps the Company manage the business better. Key activities that are relevant to this include:

- Information is collected about all aspects of customer satisfaction, including customer needs, requirements, opinions, complaints and community concerns.

- All customer information gleaned from customer visits and meetings is actioned directly, if necessary, or otherwise fed into the system through Business Unit Board Meetings.

- Information is fed back to the Customer Service MD through regular review sessions.

- Information from independently managed market research is fed directly to the executive team. This information and data are used for performance monitoring and to identify priority issues.

- Customer complaints data are assessed through the Service Failure Analysis process. This enables customer complaints to be held on computer, categorised, assessed and prioritised based on degree of severity and level of recurrence. The information is then forwarded to business unit managers, who action improvement. Where applicable, other established improvement tools, such as Six Sigma, are employed.

- To fully understand the electricity and service needs of its domestic customers, the Company recognised the changing lifestyle of people, and its market research data are differentiated into the socio-economic classifications using the MOSAIC system. This system classifies consumers into nine groups, including rural communities, low-income elders and large family suburbs.

- NIE is developing software for a CRM program, which will provide and categorise customer information in a more systematic and 'global' way and thereby turn customer information into customer knowledge that will provide innovation and learning opportunities for the Company.

14.2.3   Customer organisation

The Company is set up to enable the efficient understanding of customer issues and speedy resolution. In particular, the fact that the Company collects information from many sources means that such information must not be lost and must be acted on speedily and appropriately. The key attributes of this set-up include:

- The set-up of a Customer Services Business unit headed by a managing director. The unit comprises 13 Customer Services Centres headed by 11 Customer Services managers. The setting up of a dedicated unit not only implies that the Company recognises the importance of customer service, but also means that customer problems can be sorted out first-hand and process changes put in place very quickly.

- Key account managers have been appointed for important business clients. They are responsible for ensuring that their customers' specific needs are understood and met.

- Information on customer issues goes not only to the Customer Services Unit but also to the relevant operational personnel, including business unit managers. Regular reviews are held between key managers and the Customer Service MD to ensure that customer service information is not lost or confined to parts of the organisation.

- A customer service training programme has been implemented and delivered to all customer service employees.

- Employees are empowered to make decisions to improve customer satisfaction at their discretion. For example, customer service staff can give 'goodwill' payments of up to £100 on their own authority if a customer has been let down. Furthermore, supervisors are also encouraged to take whatever action is appropriate to sort out a customer concern.

- The number of staff at the Company's headquarters has been reduced from about 1,000 to less than 150 by moving them out to customer services centres, thereby providing closer working relationships and reducing information turnaround times.

14.3   Conclusions

NIE success at satisfying customers is based on an ability to be close enough to its customers to understand what they want. The process is then driven forward by an organisational structure and processes that enable the needs and requirements of the customers to be efficiently provided. The Company will continue to place the satisfaction of its customers at the heart of its business.

15. CASE STUDY E: AN IT COMPANY

15.1   Background

This company is one of the leading IT solutions companies in Europe, employing more than 19,200 people in 40 countries. It designs, builds and operates IT systems and services for customers across the financial services sector and the telecommunications, retail, media and government markets.

As an example, it provides e-business integration services for enterprises seeking advantage from the connected world, by drawing upon its extensive experience of delivering fully quantified and incremental business benefits. The services provided include new media design, consultancy and systems integration, as well as managed infrastructure services. All these underpin the mission-critical requirements of businesses.

15.2   Customer Satisfaction Approach

The Company has been particularly active with respect to responding to customer enquiries and monitoring performance. It has adopted an inclusive approach, which in some cases has been underpinned by the use of benchmarking techniques.

15.2.1   Responding to customer enquiries

In the summer of 1999, a project was started with the aim of improving the way in which customer enquiries were handled. Three issues, in particular, were identified and focused on:

1. Taking initial information from customers – the Company had an inconsistent way of getting information from customers/prospective customers when enquiries were made. As a result, a decision was made to improve the existing centralised help desk significantly to ensure greater consistency. A benchmarking exercise with a motoring organisation helped to improve the existing processes.

2. The relevant department/person to direct enquiries to – it was important to direct customer enquiries/questions to the right person and to ensure that such enquiries did not get lost in the system. In an effort to identify good practice, the Company carried out a benchmarking exercise with organisations that directed enquiries on a routine basis. The two types of organisation chosen were libraries and hospitals because of their abilities to direct queries to the right person using a disparate set of data.

3. How to deliver disappointing news to customers – delivering disappointing news to customers is an important but often overlooked aspect of customer relationship development. Disappointing news is not usually a result of poor performance by the company. It is usually the type of news that means that a customer's information system will need to be replaced or repaired or modified. This will typically have some cost implications for the customers and may even mean that their systems may be unable to function during the repair/replacement process. This will clearly be disappointing news for the customer and needs to be delivered with care. In order to facilitate this, the Company benchmarked itself against the methods used by hospital consultants who often have to give bad news to patients and/or patients' relatives. The exercise produced a number of steps for delivering disappointing news and the Company has adapted this. The primary steps as used by hospital consultants delivering news to the patient/relative are:
   – ask if the patient/relative understands what has been said
   – repeat the news to the patient/relative
   – ask if the patient/relative has anything to say
   – explain to the patient/relative the background to the situation and then outline the steps that the hospital, doctor and/or patient will have to take.

The adaption of this process has led to more directness with customers. Customers appreciated this openness and being open has now been emphasised as a significant corporate value.

15.2.2   Monitoring performance

The company has developed highly structured approaches to monitoring its customer satisfaction performance and employee recognition. The main aspects of this approach are as follows:

CSIP (eCSIP) – The customer satisfaction interview programme (CSIP) is carried out by a third party organisation on behalf of the Company. The interview is carried out with a senior manager in a key/strategic company against a defined set of questions. One or two interviews per customer are carried out yearly and the programme currently applies to about 100 customers. Actions identified from the individual interview are agreed with the customers and then carried out. For physically remote customers, an electronic version of the programme (eCSIP) is applied.

Customer Satisfaction Survey – These are carried out at a lower level than the CSIP. The survey consists of ten business-related questions and can be used by any function in the organisation, including project, service, construction and sales functions. Results from the survey are typically used within the divisions and summarised for the group review.

Service Performance – These are monitored internally against defined Service Level Agreements. Specific customer problems are tracked through a company-wide issues database, which classifies problems into four categories according to customer impact.

Customer Satisfaction Reviews – On a quarterly basis, the group reviews the overall performance of the Company's divisions. The quarterly review examines how well the Company is performing, identifies trends and examines the overall effect on the business.

Internal Excellence Scheme – The internal excellence scheme is a means of recognising employees for a job well done. Although the scheme is not specifically for customer satisfaction performance, some of the selection criteria are related to customer relationships. The scheme works through nominations by managers, and the nominees are then assessed against set criteria, which consist of role model behaviour, knowledge sharing, delighting customers, effective people and boosting margins. Depending on the evaluation performance, a nominee is then awarded a gold, silver or bronze award. Silver and bronze awards can be awarded by the different businesses while the group gives gold awards yearly. Award winners are given a plaque and small gifts.

15.3   Summary

The approach to customer satisfaction adopted by the Company stands out in two ways. The first is the use of benchmarking methods to understand underlying customer satisfaction principles that can be applied to its operations. The second is the quarterly review of customer satisfaction performance. Many companies tend to review performance on an annual basis, but the quarterly review means that the Company is much closer to its key/strategic customers, and any individual issues and/or trends are identified early and can be addressed effectively.

16. CASE STUDY F: KRAFT FOODS

16.1   Background

Kraft Foods is part of Philip Morris, the world's second largest food company. With operations in 140 countries and 117,000 employees, Kraft Foods produces some of the best-known food brands, including Jacobs, Philadelphia, Maxwell House, Nabisco and Suchard. The Company has a total of more than 65 brands across five core sectors – snacks, beverages, cheese, grocery and convenient meals.

Kraft Foods UK Ltd is the UK operation of the parent company and has its headquarters at Cheltenham, with its main factory in Banbury. The UK customers range from major retailers to independent wholesalers and cash-and-carry operations. Kraft has been active in the development of customer satisfaction initiatives and the Company's vision is to attain legendary service tailored to meet each client's specific needs. In the recent past, the Company has won an Institute of Grocery Distribution (IGD) award for its customer service performance.

16.2   Service Excellence Model

The customer service team at Kraft has developed a service excellence model, which comprises the following attributes:

- Variant management – providing substitutions needs or introducing promotions
- Delivery interface – efficient and secure transfer of inventory
- Data alignment – ensuring that information is up to date and regularly cross-checked

- Seasonal planning – providing for seasonally influenced fluctuations in demand
- Customer satisfaction – working with customers to record and manage feedback, including complaints
- Knowledge exchange – a greater understanding of processes
- Great people – having personnel who are dedicated to and passionate about customer service
- Perfect ordering – ensuring that customer orders are error-free.

In order to assess its performance against these criteria and competitor performance, the Company carried out a survey of its customers in 1999.

16.2.1 The survey

The key objectives of the survey included an understanding of customer expectations in the Kraft supply chain, measuring satisfaction against these expectations and identifying areas for improvement. The survey covered a broad range of customers and was primarily carried out over the phone since Kraft wanted verbatim comments.

A total of 112 customers was initially contacted by means of a posted flyer informing of the survey, its purpose and the mechanisms to be used. A week after posting, a member of Kraft staff telephoned to arrange an appointment or carry out the survey, if convenient, at the time. Respondents were also offered an option of completing the survey by post or e-mail. Of the 112 companies initially contacted, 74 completed the exercise, with more than 90% using the telephone option. Respondents were also asked if and how they wanted feedback from the study.

Kraft's customer services and logistics management teams analysed the survey both quantitatively and qualitatively. Overall, customers perceived Kraft as very good, but there was room for improvement. The worst score was better than 'good', although the respondents indicated that none of their suppliers consistently provided outstanding service.

The survey also gave a clear indication of how Kraft compared with its competitors, and this feedback helped the Company develop its strategic plans for the next year. In particular, the survey showed that Kraft needed to improve on delivery interface, variant management and data alignment.

16.3 Improvement Actions

The feedback from the survey was posted on the Company Intranet, and feedback packs were sent to more than 90% of respondents, of which 78% were willing to discuss results in meetings and agree future actions.

Kraft recognised the need to improve communication across the supply chain and identify the different needs and expectations of its different customer groups. A detailed breakdown of the survey results was sent to key personnel in the supply chain function, and a presentation given to all supply chain personnel at a quarterly review meeting.

Subsequently, a number of initiatives to improve performance were started. These included:

- A drop 'n' drive process, which replaced on-the-spot checking of deliveries. This implied a high degree of trust between Kraft and its customers.

- Improved use of communication technology, including e-mail and electronic data interchange (EDI).

- Improved lead times and consolidated deliveries.

- Project perfect order – a re-engineering of the order processes, involving customer input, advance notification of despatch and installation of phone in delivery vehicles to enable communication of delays.

- Development of a set of new training programmes to develop skill sets required to support the drive for improvement. The training programmes varied in content and purpose and included the following:
  - skills to enable customer-facing staff ensure effective meetings with customers
  - a review of the service excellence model for updates and improvements
  - service excellence workshops for all members of the customer services team to ensure full understanding of the model and its application.
  - quarterly workshops to address the specific needs of the team

16.4 Conclusions

The service excellence model and the associated survey have provided Kraft Foods with a unique platform for improving its customer service performance. Although the overall indication was that Kraft was very good, areas for improvement were also identified, thus giving the Company a new set of targets. In order to ensure continuity and sustainability, all service excellence initiatives are reviewed regularly and a CD-ROM is being produced for internal staff training and external customer awareness. Finally, the Company plans to carry out future customer surveys.

17. CASE STUDY G: THE BENCHMARKING CLUB FOR THE FOOD AND DRINKS INDUSTRY

17.1   Introduction

The Benchmarking Club for the food and drinks industry was set up in 1997 with the support of MAFF (now DEFRA). The Club was led and managed by Leatherhead Food RA (LFRA), one of the world's leading research, consultancy, information and training centres for the food industry. The Club was set up to be a common interest group and a forum to enable its members to share best practice. In the 4 years to 2001, the Club boasted a membership of some of the leading food and drinks companies in the UK, including Campbell's Soups, Dromona Quality Foods, Smithkline Beecham Consumer Products, Van den Bergh Foods, J.A. Sharwood's and Co., Seaforth Corn Mills, J. Sainsbury's Supermarkets, Kraft Jacobs Suchard, Scottish Courage Brands, HP Foods Ltd, Glanbia Foods Ltd and Mckey Food Service.

The members of the group recognised the importance of customer satisfaction and decided to set up a customer satisfaction workgroup to examine the practice of customer satisfaction in greater detail. The group, which was led and managed by Leatherhead Food RA, consisted of customer service managers from four of the member companies. Having a sub-group of specialists was beneficial as it enabled a larger resource pool of people that had day-to-day contact with customers.

17.2   Approach

The group carried out the project over a period of 6 months with the overall objective of identifying best practice in customer satisfaction. A number of workshops were held to focus on various aspects of customer satisfaction. The activities used by the sub-group were:

- Each member of the group gave a presentation of personal experiences of good and poor customer service.

- The approach adopted by each of the four companies in the group was profiled.

- Each member of the group carried out a case study of a best practice company. The best practice companies were chosen from winners of business excellence awards and were mostly non-food companies.

- Findings from each case study were fed back to the group and these, as well as the individual approaches and experiences, formed the basis for the discussions of the group.

- In applying lessons from the various sources, the group was careful to ensure that the focus was on the underlying principles that support customer satisfaction rather than the indicator activities.

17.3   Findings

The discussions within the group indicated that it was not possible to define a standard list of measures for customer satisfaction. The measures to be used for customer satisfaction are influenced by such factors as customer type, product type and characteristics, and pre-determined service level agreements (SLAs).

It was also recognised that satisfaction is transient in nature and, as customer expectation and choice increase, offering the same levels of service or applying the same measures may not lead to the same level of satisfaction. Companies need to improve their offering consistently if they are to maintain or improve the levels of satisfaction that they give to their customers.

The group noted that some organisations judged the satisfaction of their customers using only internal knowledge supported by indicators. This can be misleading as indicators such as repeat purchase may reflect the lack of a suitable alternative product rather than the fact that the customer is happy with the company's products or service. The input of the customer needs to be sought when determining levels of satisfaction.

Although there is no prescriptive route to achieving customer satisfaction, the study of best practice companies showed that there are certain principles that organisations need to understand and implement in their own way to facilitate customer satisfaction. These are:

- Understanding the customer – It is important to identify with the business of each customer and understand how to add value for them. Different customers would have different needs, which need to be identified and fulfilled.

- Organisation – Company processes and the organisational structure and focus should be directed towards making the customers satisfied. This would involve examining production and supplier strategies, training, company mission, etc.

- Communication – Internal and external communication needs to be effective and streamlined. In particular, communication with customers should not be concentrated mainly on sales and cost-related issues, but should include after-sales communication, joint improvement projects, etc.

- Product – The actual product or service delivered by the company needs to meet the required characteristics in terms of functionality, quality, presentation, etc.

- People – It is important that employees within the company are customer-focused. This should apply not just to the customer-facing employees but to everyone within the company as it is important for the whole organisation to appreciate the importance of the customer.

- Agents of dissatisfaction – These are factors that in themselves may not lead to satisfaction but whose absence may lead to customer dissatisfaction. Companies need to be aware of these factors and take steps to accommodate them. These factors could include poor labelling, non-identification of allergy-inducing foods, and ethical considerations in the food chain.

17.4   Summary

The project provided the participating companies with an understanding of the fundamental principles of customer satisfaction. This provided a platform for the companies to enhance their approaches to customer service and satisfaction individually, and also to understand what factors to take into consideration in designing future customer service initiatives.

PART 3: CUSTOMER SATISFACTION IMPROVEMENT TOOLKIT

18. INTRODUCTION

The aim of this toolkit is to provide organisations with a basis for the development and improvement of their customer-related practices. It is intended as a general guide only and not as a prescriptive tool. For this reason, the toolkit is divided into three sections, which represent the commonly accepted generic steps to customer satisfaction. The three sections are:

- Understanding the customer
- Understanding your organisation
- Delivering to the customer

These three steps are strategic stages of improving customer satisfaction. For each of these, the toolkit provides a breakdown to mini-project level activities. Companies may adapt these to their organisations. It is not possible to provide specific tasks for these projects as the toolkit then becomes too prescriptive and will fail to add value to a substantial proportion of the organisations that intend to use it.

A brief description of the three topics and their relevance is given below.

Understanding the customer. This is the first thing an organisation that wishes to improve customer satisfaction should do. Understanding the customer involves knowing your product, your competitors' products, the section of the market you wish to target (e.g. value-conscious, quality-leaning, service-oriented) and the key account customers you would wish to develop.

Understanding your organisation. Understanding the customers and what they want provides an opportunity for the organisation to look inwards to determine whether it has the capabilities to deliver these requirements. It also needs to determine whether these requirements are in line with its strategic plans before taking action to ensure that these strategies are deployed and devolved throughout the organisation.

<u>Delivering to the customer</u>. This involves ensuring that the deployed strategies are turned into positive action that adds value for the customers and thus provides the company with a potential base of core and loyal customers. This stage also involves an evaluation of customer perception of the organisation, the building of relationships and trust and the development of partnerships and mutually beneficial joint improvement efforts.

Team development

It is suggested that the exercises in this toolkit be carried out by a multi-functional team of between three and six people depending on the organisation's culture and structure (e.g. size, number of products, size of market/customer base). A multi-functional approach has the advantage of taking into account views and inputs from different parts of the organisation. Furthermore, any decisions reached would have a wide-based ownership and would be more likely to be successfully implemented.

It is recommended that the toolkit implementation process should be led by a facilitator. Guidance notes for the facilitator are presented in this toolkit. Ideally, the facilitator should:

- have a good broad appreciation of the business
- have a dynamic and pragmatic disposition
- have good communication and presentation skills
- be respected within the company

It is hoped that you will find the material in this toolkit useful and easily adaptable to your organisation. It is worth noting that it will take patience and planning to achieve a high level of customer satisfaction and loyalty and it is advisable for each organisation to proceed at a speed and level of detail that suits its circumstances. Some organisations may find that some parts of the toolkit are more relevant to their current level of development than others and may find it more beneficial to focus only on the sections that are closest to their needs.

Roadmap and example

A roadmap that illustrates the suggested improvement process and the expected output at each stage is presented at the start of the toolkit. Furthermore, completed example tools are presented at the end of the toolkit.

18.1 Facilitator Notes

The broad aims of the facilitator are to manage the team, ensure that it remains focused, achieve consensus with wide ownership of solutions on all issues, and lead team discussions. It is not expected that the facilitator will have solutions to all the issues that would be raised.

As the facilitator, you may choose the members of the team or be involved in an already established team. However, it is important that the team members possess the following:

- ability and willingness to discuss honestly and openly
- ability to accept different views from other members of the team
- willingness to reach consensus with other team members
- objectivity in their opinions
- an understanding of the relevant business processes and activities of the organisation.

Furthermore, as the facilitator, you should ensure that any agreed actions are owned by all members and led/implemented by specified individuals. You are also responsible for setting the date and time of meetings and for informing the team members. The following guidelines would help during team meetings.

- Brief the team members on the need for the exercise and the process to be followed.
- Inform the members how you intend to manage the process.
- Remind them to be honest, open, dispassionate and receptive to opposing views.
- Work through the process in a pre-determined sequence.
- Ensure that consensus decisions are agreed by all team members.
- Ensure agreed action plans are well defined and owned by specific individuals.
- At the end of the session, map the plans to the original objectives of the team.

18.2 The Roadmap

The following roadmap gives an overview of the tools provided in this section and gives an indication of the expected output from the different tools.

CUSTOMER SATISFACTION

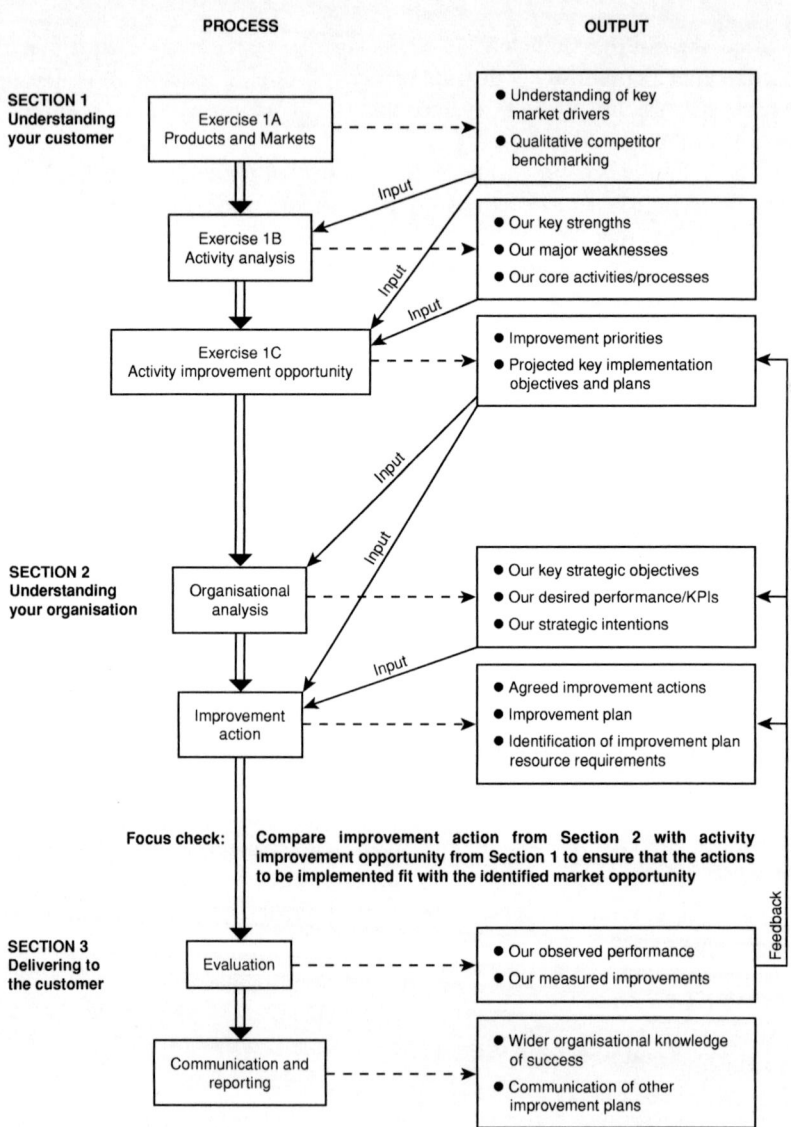

The roadmap

19. SECTIONS OF TOOLKIT

19.1   Section 1 – Understanding your Customer

19.1.1   Product and markets – Exercise 1A

1   OUR PRODUCTS
- Have we identified our key products?
- What are they?
- Have we identified our supplementary products?
- What are they?
- Is service delivery recognised as part of our product offering?
- If yes, what are our key service delivery attributes (e.g. technical support, after-sales service, delivery management)?
- If no, is there any reason why service delivery should not be part of our product offering?

2   MARKET AND CUSTOMERS
- For each of our products, what market do we service in terms of
  - Value?
  - Size?
  - Geographical location?
  - Service delivery?
- Is this the market we ideally want to service?
- For each of our products, who are our key customers?
- Do we know what attributes our customers consider to be most important or value most?

- Are we their key supplier for
  - one product only
  - a variety of products
- For how long have we been their supplier?
- What percentage of their purchases do we supply?
- Over the last 2 years, has our level of trade with key customers increased or decreased?
  - By what margin?
- Has the global/national/regional market for our products increased or decreased?
  - By what margin?
- What other companies that are currently not customers or key customers are major users of our product type?
- Do we want them to become customers?
- Are their any restrictions stopping them from becoming customers (e.g. geographical constraints, confidentiality agreements with current customers)?

3   OUR COMPETITORS

- What are our key competing products?
- Are our products differentiated from competing products?
- In what way?
- If our products are not differentiated, do they need to be?
- Can they be differentiated (including service delivery)?
- Do our product differentiation attributes converge with the customer preference attributes identified in section 2 above?
- Do we need to revise our product attributes?
- Which product(s) lead(s) the market?

4   SUMMARY

- What are the key learning points from this exercise?
- What are our priority areas?
- Which of these can we accomplish easily (quick wins)?
- Other comments

19.1.2   What we do – Exercise 1B

This exercise enables the organisation to run a relatively quick check of current activities aimed at understanding the customer. When used in conjunction with exercise 1A, it helps to validate the answers given in that exercise.

Make each of the following suggested activities and sub-activities a subject of the form provided below. You may also use other activities that are relevant to your organisation and its operations.

1. Customer understanding
    - Use of customer questionnaire surveys
    - Use of telephone surveys
    - Use of key account managers
    - Use of published information (trade journals, conferences, etc.)
    - Direct meetings with customers/potential customers
    - Development and documentation of customer profiles and preferences

2. Market knowledge
    - Use of independent market researchers
    - Use of mystery shoppers
    - Knowledge or relevant emerging technologies
    - In-house marketing analysis
    - access to specialist marketing information (reports, etc.)

3. Competitor evaluation
    - Competitor product evaluation
    - Competitor service evaluation
    - Customer's/potential customer's perception of competitor product/service
    - Competitor marketing strategy/product positioning
    - Other competitor development (e.g. new products/technology)

4. Own product evaluation
    - Own product evaluation
    - Own service evaluation
    - Customer's/potential customer's perception of own product/service
    - In-house marketing strategy/product positioning
    - Other in-house development (e.g. new products/technology)

Activity Analysis Form

Name of activity
Who is responsible for this activity?
How often is it carried out?
Can the result/performance be measured?
What measures are used?
Who carries out the measurements?
What are the measures/information used for?
Who is responsible for reviewing the effectiveness of this activity?
When was this activity last reviewed?
What can we do to improve this activity?

19.1.3   What we want to do – Exercise 1C

Exercises 1A and 1B should have given a clear indication of the issues the organisation needs to address in the short, medium and long term. This short exercise will assist in documenting and prioritising those issues. The completed output from this exercise will be used in the next section, which focuses on knowing your organisation.

For each of the identified improvement areas, complete the following form.

Activity Improvement Opportunity Form

Name of activity	
What needs to be improved?	
How can this be done?	
Priority rating	**Implementation timeframe**
Department/person with overall responsibility	
Cost of implementation (financial and human)	
Desired output	
How output will be measured	
Person to measure output	
Implementation review milestones	

Section summary

By the end of this section, your organisation should have an understanding of its markets and customers. In addition, the positioning of its products in comparison with competitors' and customer requirements should be understood. A picture of what the company needs to focus on should now be emerging.

19.2   Section 2 – Understanding your Organisation

Having identified what the market wants and what its key areas of focus are, the organisation now needs to look inwards to understand its current direction, its strengths, weaknesses and how these link with the issues identified in section 1.

The organisational analysis grid presented in this section provides a tool to assist organisations understand their operations and link these to what they have identified as important for their market and customers.

The grid provided in this section is provided only as a guide and is not intended to be prescriptive. All companies need to define the contents of their own organisational grid in relation to their unique needs and aspirations.

Organisational Analysis Grid

Factor	Test	Objective (strategic/operational)	Action/Comments
Strategy			
Deployment			
People			
Customers			
Processes			
Resources			
Other			
Other			
Other			

Note:
- The 'test' column should be used to determine the level of performance of the organisation in qualitative and/or quantitative terms
- The 'objective' should describe what the company aims to achieve as defined in its corporate plans and/or identified from section 1
- The 'action/comments' column should convey a decision on whether (based on section 1 and previous columns) this is a factor the company needs to improve, delay, redesign, etc.
- Each factor that the company decides needs improvement now needs to be evaluated in some more detail using the 'Improvement action' form overleaf.

Improvement action

Overall objective (and priority rating)	Specific actions to be taken	
Measures of success		Key impact on customers
Commencement date of improvement activity		Projected completion date
Improvement milestones	Project leader/owner	Executive sponsor
Impact on current operational activities		
Financial resources required	Human resources required	Resources approved by executive sponsor
Other comments		

As a means of validation, the completed 'Improvement action' form may be compared with the 'Activity Improvement opportunity' form presented in section 1. This gives the organisation an opportunity to see how the original ideas generated from understanding customer needs have evolved of changed.

19.3   Section 3 – Delivering to the Customer

From the previous two sections, your organisation should have identified, and started taking action to improve activities that lead to customer satisfaction. The last important steps to take are to monitor satisfaction and promote customer relationships through the adoption of added-value principles such as partnerships. To facilitate this form of development, this section provides two sets of tools/guidelines:

1.   Generic evaluation of customer satisfaction performance. This would give an overview of the overall progress the organisation has made as a result of its improvement actions. Where desirable, it may also be applied to individual customers. As much as possible, this should be cross-referenced with the 'milestones' identified in the 'Improvement action' form in section 2.

2. Customer added-value opportunities. This may be used where the organisation has identified or wishes to investigate the ability to form closer relationships with identified customers or groups of customers. It is likely that, in most instances, key individual customers would be evaluated independently.

19.3.1 Generic evaluation of customer satisfaction

To enable the organisation to monitor this, it needs to define its means of measurement and how its is reported.

19.3.1.1 Measurement methods

The following grid, which takes the form of a tick list, may be used to define measurement methods. To ensure that no activity gets left out, all activities for which an 'Improvement action' form is generated in section 2 should automatically be added to the list.

	Development/evaluation method				
Action/company objective (e.g. from Improvement Action form)	Customer surveys	Customer visits	Balanced scorecard	Complaints record	Other
On-time delivery					
After-sales follow-up					
Invoicing accuracy					
Contact with key account manager					
Product returns reduction					
Other					
Other					
Other					

Note:
The development/evaluation methods and company objectives in the above grid are presented as an example only and do not reflect the wide range of options that are available or are being used by organisations. For each organisation, the final constitution of the grid will depend on its individual circumstances.

19.3.1.2   Reporting and communication

The results measured need to be communicated systematically to the right people within the organisation. To enable this, the following need to be addressed:

- Who/which department will results be provided to? (e.g. production, accounts, directors)
- What level of detail will be presented to each group?
- Who will take responsibility for producing and delivering the results?
- How regularly will results be presented?
- Who will collect, collate and analyse corrective/improvement suggestions from these groups?
- Who will be responsible for carrying out/monitoring any corrective/ improvement actions resulting?

It would be expected that, once these issues have been addressed initially, a pattern will be established and will thus become part of normal working principle. For example, the board will become accustomed to receiving quarterly customer satisfaction results in the same way that they receive monthly sales figures.

19.3.2   Customer added value

Organisations that have developed and deliver efficient and effective customer-related processes and performance could seek to enhance the relationships they have with their customers. Such relationships should, ideally, lead to some measurable benefits for both supplier and customer. Some of the key reasons why organisations develop such relationships are as follows:

- Improvement of service to customers
- Improving customer loyalty
- Further improvement in operational performance
- Reduction of cost base across a range of functions such as purchasing, distribution, inventory and R&D
- Medium- to long-term strategic planning
- Technological development

Added-value relationships are generally developed with individual customers rather than with the whole customer base, particularly where the organisation has a wide customer base with varying requirements and needs.

It is important that both organisations derive mutually agreeable or even equitable benefits from the relationship rather than one party (in most cases the customer) enjoying (and sometimes dictating) the benefits almost exclusively.

19.3.2.1   How are partnerships formed?

Partnerships typically start with one party identifying a need or an opportunity, or facing a significant problem and deciding to approach the other party with the aim of working closely together. There is an assumption that, based on past association or reputation, the initiating partner believes that its proposed associate has or can develop the ability to achieve the intended goals. To a certain extent, this means understanding the business of the proposed partner. The following guidelines give an idea of issues to be considered in the development of added-value partnerships. The guidelines are generic in nature and can be used by either the customer or the supplier. They can be applied to one customer (or supplier) or a specific group of customers (or suppliers).

Guidelines for added-value partnerships

Partnership stage/issue	Examples
Determine areas of your business where you could develop partnerships or where there is an opportunity	• Development of a new range of products • Combining purchasing power on basic raw materials • Bulk purchase/negotiation of advertising space, business travel discounts, etc. • Joint development of novel packaging technology • Preferred supplier/customer status • Product delivery strategies
Identify potential partner organisations	• Customer/supplier with a gap in product range • Customer/supplier with a tendency for innovation • Customer/supplier in special circumstances (e.g. constant travelling to and from long distance organisation could lead to the negotiation of discount fares with a particular airline) • Third party that can provide a complementary product (e.g. supermarkets have partnerships with banks, insurance companies, travel agents, etc.

CUSTOMER SATISFACTION

Partnership stage/issue	Examples
Quantify proposed benefits of partnerships of both parties	• Expected sales of new products • Improvement in on-time, in-full delivery • Exclusivity and technological advantage over competitors • Long-term supply contract • Development of personnel skills • 20% reduction in stockholding costs
Approach potential partner(s)	• Directly contact relevant function within the proposed partner organisation • 'Sound out' the idea by using other contacts within the company • Approach at board/senior executive level • Approach through a third party/agent
Arrange meetings with the potential partner	• Identify the lead individuals in both organisations • Decide the best time to hold meeting • Hold series of meetings until both parties are happy to proceed
Quantify and agree benefits to both parties	• This may be agreed in principle or written down • Agree how benefits would be shared
Agree level at which partnerships would be operated	• Board level • Operational level (e.g. supplier warehouse and customer depot) • Departmental/sectional level (e.g. new invoicing process)
Agree the nature of the partnership	• Formal documented partnership • Single project of continuous partnership • Fixed term/renewable partnership • Exclusive, confidential partnership • Agree Intellectual Property Rights ownership
Agree review process	• Determine how regularly partnership would be reviewed at operational/strategic levels • Determine individuals/functions responsible for review • Determine measures of success • Agree procedures for termination of partnership, if necessary
Communicate, train and commence	• Communicate partnership agreement to all relevant personnel in both organisations • Where required, train directly affected employees in necessary skills to effect partnership • Communicate partnership and benefits to relevant external parties (e.g. consumers)

19.4 Overview

The tools in this chapter have been developed to give organisations a helping hand, and suggestions for improvement for all levels of organisational development and across a broad spectrum of customer-satisfaction-related issues.

The tools are presented in an order that encourages organisations to improve customer satisfaction from the bottom up (i.e. focus on getting the basics right first). The tools, however, do not include some common concepts such as designing and administering customer satisfaction questionnaires, conducting telephone surveys, etc. Although mention was made of some of these methodologies (e.g. under measurement methods in section 2), there is a wide range of publications and organisations that are available to assist organisations in this respect (see references and sources of information, p157).

While most of the case studies presented in this book are from the food industry, the lessons learnt from them and the tools developed and presented in Part 3 are applicable to organisations in a range of industries – service or manufacturing.

It is hoped that the information presented in this book will go some way to assisting organisations develop that most desired but often elusive goal – customer-satisfaction-enabled loyalty.

20. EXAMPLE TOOLKIT

This section gives an example of how some of the tools presented in Part 3 could look when completed. It is intended to be used as an aid for the effective application of the toolkit.

20.1   Section 1 – Understanding your Customer

20.1.1   *Product and markets – Exercise 1A*

1   OUR PRODUCTS

- Have we identified our key products?
Yes

- What are they?
Products A, B and C

- Have we identified our supplementary products?
Yes

- What are they?
Products X and Y

- Is service delivery recognised as part of our product offering?
No

- If yes, what are our key service delivery attributes (e.g. technical support, after-sales service, delivery management)?
N/A

- If no, is there any reason why service delivery should not be part of our product offering?

No – we should consider our service delivery as part of our product offering. This could provide us with a competitive edge

2 MARKET AND CUSTOMERS

- For each of our products, what market do we service in terms of
  - *Value? Product A - premium market (etc. for other products)*
  - *Size? Product A - 65,000 cases per year*
  - *Geographical location? UK only*
  - *Service delivery? 4 days lead time, Warehouse delivery*

- Is this the market we ideally want to service?

Yes

- For each of our products, who are our key customers?

Products A&B – supermarkets, Product Y – caterers, etc.

- Do we know what attributes our customers consider to be most important or value most?

No

- Are we their key supplier for
  - one product only *Customers 1 and 2*
  - a variety of products *Customers 3 and 4*

- For how long have we been their supplier?

Customer 1 (2 years), customer 3 (15 years), etc.

- What percentage of their purchases do we supply?

Customer 1 (25%), customer 2 (65%), etc.

- Over the last 2 years, has our level of trade with key customers increased or decreased?

Increased

  - By what margin?

Customer 3 (10% or £30K), etc.

- Has the global/national/regional market for our products increased or decreased?
Increased for product A nationally, unchanged for product B, etc.

  - By what margin?
Product A (3%), Product B (0%)

- What other companies that are currently not customers or key customers are major users of our product type?
Wholesalers, independent distributors, hotel chains

- Do we want them to become customers?
Yes

- Are their any restrictions stopping them from becoming customers (e.g. geographical constraints, confidentiality agreements with current customers)?
No fundamental restrictions

3 OUR COMPETITORS

- What are our key competing products?
Products I,J,K,L,M

- Are our products differentiated from competing products?
Yes, for products B and X

- In what way?
Quality, innovative packaging, ease of use

- If our products are not differentiated, do they need to be?
Yes

- Can they be differentiated (including service delivery)?
Yes

- Do our product differentiation attributes converge with the customer preference attributes identified in section 2 above?

N/A

- Do we need to revise our product attributes?

Yes

- Which product(s) lead the market?

Products Y, B, K, L

4 SUMMARY

- What are the key learning points from this exercise?

We need to consider service delivery improvement generally and differentiation for some of our products

- What are our priority areas?

Product delivery
Communication
Complaints handling
Product quality
Non-GM products

- Which of these can we accomplish easily (quick wins)?

Communication
Complaints handling

- Other comments

Improvement in these two areas can be made with minimal cost implications but we need to re-examine our customer development strategy in the medium term.

20.1.2   What we do – Exercise 1B

This exercise enables the organisation to run a relatively quick check of current activities aimed at understanding the customer. When used in conjunction with exercise 1A, it helps to validate the answers given in that exercise.

Make each of the following suggested activities and sub-activities a subject of the form provided below. You may also use other activities that are relevant to your organisation and its operations.

1. Customer understanding
    - Use of customer questionnaire surveys
    - Use of telephone surveys
    - Use of key account managers
    - Use of published information (trade journals, conferences, etc.)
    - Direct meetings with customers/potential customers
    - Development and documentation of customer profiles and preferences

2. Market knowledge
    - Use of independent market researchers
    - Use of mystery shoppers
    - Knowledge or relevant emerging technologies
    - In-house marketing analysis
    - Access to specialist marketing information (reports, etc.)

3. Competitor evaluation
    - Competitor product evaluation
    - Competitor service evaluation
    - Customer's/potential customer's perception of competitor product/service
    - Competitor marketing strategy/product positioning
    - Other competitor development (e.g. new products/technology)

4. Own product evaluation
    - Own product evaluation
    - Own service evaluation
    - Customer's/potential customer's perception of own product/service
    - In-house marketing strategy/product positioning
    - Other in-house development (e.g. new products/technology)

Activity Analysis Form

Name of activity: *Meetings with customers and potential customers*

Who is responsible for this activity? *Sales team only*

How often is it carried out? *Variable*

Can the result/performance be measured? *Usually*

What measures are used? *No. of visits per customer, sales value*

Who carries out the measurements? *Sales managers*

What are the measures/information used for? *Monitoring of sales per customer, sales commissions, sales strategy development*

Who is responsible for reviewing the effectiveness of this activity? *Sales and Commercial Director*

When was this activity last reviewed? *Reviewed quarterly*

What can we do to improve this activity? *Develop alternative methods of contacting customers, improve customer contact with other departments, develop new measures of effectiveness*

20.1.3   What we want to do – Exercise 1C

Exercises 1A and 1B should have given a clear indication of the issues the organisation needs to address in the short, medium and long term. This short exercise will assist in documenting and prioritising those issues. the completed output from this exercise will be used in the next section, which focuses on knowing your organisation.

For each of the identified improvement areas, complete the following form.

Activity Improvement Opportunity Form

Name of activity: *Customer contact*	
What needs to be improved? *Level, frequency and quality of contact with customer and potential customers*	
How can this be done? *Encourage executive level contact, develop joint problem-solving/product development teams with customers, improve contact through the use of technology*	
Priority rating: *High*	**Implementation time frame:** *8 weeks*
Department/person with overall responsibility: *Sales and Marketing Director*	
Cost of implementation (financial and human): *15% of senior managers time, £15K (estimated) for training courses*	
Desired output: *Better quality interaction with customers to cross-sell products*	
How output will be measured: *Current measures plus amount of senior management time spent with customers, estimated increase in use of e-mails, video conferencing, etc., value of new products cross-sold to existing customers*	
Implementation review milestones: *Monthly for first 6 months and then quarterly*	

Section summary

By the end of this section, your organisation should have an understanding of its markets and customers. In addition, the positioning of its products in comparison with competitors' and customer requirements should be understood. A picture of what the company needs to focus on should now be emerging.

20.2   Section 2 – Understanding your Organisation

Having identified what the market wants and what its key areas of focus are, the organisation now needs to look inwards to understand its current direction, its strengths, weaknesses and how these link with the issues identified in section 1.

The organisational analysis grid presented in this section provides a tool to assist organisations understand their operations and link this to what they have identified as important for their market and customers.

The grid provided in this section is provided only as a guide and is not intended to be prescriptive. All companies need to define the contents of their own organisational grid in relation to their unique needs and aspirations.

Organisational Analysis Grid

Factor	Test	Objective (strategic/ operational)	Action/Comments
Strategy			
Deployment			
People			
Customers			
Processes			
Resources			
Technology	% of staff with access to e-mail; no. of customers visiting staff with PDAs, mobile phones, etc.	The company has no well-defined technological objectives	Develop strategic approach to use of technology; define plan to facilitate deployment of technology
Marketing	No. and value of promotions annually, road shows and trade fairs attended, advertising budget, etc.	To improve customer/ consumer awareness of our products, to understand emerging customer needs, etc.	Maintain current momentum and keep alert for new marketing initiatives
Other			

Note

- The 'test' column should be used to determine the level of performance of the organisation in qualitative and/or quantitative terms
- The 'objective' should describe what the company aims to achieve as defined in its corporate plans and/or identified from section 1
- The 'action/comments' column should convey a decision on whether (based on section 1 and previous columns) this is a factor the company needs to improve, delay, redesign, etc.
- Each factor that the company decides needs improvement now needs to be evaluated in some more detail using the 'Improvement action' form below.

Improvement action

Overall objective (and priority rating): *Improved communication with customers; this will be given a high priority*

Specific actions to be taken: *Senior managers to have at least one meeting a month with similar executive in a potential customer company; marketing team to initiate joint customer visits with salesmen; all off-site representatives to be provided with computers that enable access to company network, etc.*

Measures of success: *Level of uptake of new initiatives, no. of customer visits carried out by executives, etc.*

Key impact on customers: *Increased visibility of our company, better informed representatives, more strategic high level contact, quicker resolution of problems*

Commencement date of improvement activity: *Relevant training to be carried out over the next month. Six-month trial to start on 1 August*

Projected completion date: *Activities to be continuous until otherwise advised*

Improvement milestones: *£50K in sales to new customers within 6 weeks of trial commencement. Completed training for all executives within the next 3 weeks, etc.*

Project leader/owner: *To be held jointly by marketing manager and training manager*

Executive sponsor: *Managing Director*

Impact on current operational activities: *Increased demand on executive time (time management and delegation to be considered); more internal meetings between sales, marketing and IT departments, etc.*

Financial resources required: *£17.5K for training, £10K for computer and other communications equipment, etc.*

Human resources required: *20% of executive time, 10% of marketing team's time, 2 sales executives to be recruited*

Resources approved by executive sponsor: *£35K*

Other comments: *Weekly progress reports to be given to executive sponsor*

As a means of validation, the completed 'Improvement action' form may be compared with the 'Activity improvement opportunity' form presented in section 1. This gives the organisation an opportunity to see how the original ideas generated from understanding customer needs have evolved or changed.

20.3 Section 3 – Delivering to the Customer

From the previous two sections, your organisation should have identified and started taking action to improve activities that lead to customer satisfaction. The last important steps to take are to monitor satisfaction and promote customer relationships through the adoption of added-value principles such as partnerships.

To facilitate this form of development, this section provides two sets of tools/guidelines:

1. Generic evaluation of customer satisfaction performance. This would give an overview of the overall progress the organisation has made as a result of its improvement actions. Where desirable, it may also be applied to individual customers. As much as possible, this should be cross-referenced with the 'milestones' identified in the 'Improvement action' form in section 2.

2. Customer added-value opportunities. This may be used where the organisation has identified or wishes to investigate the ability to form closer relationships with identified customers or groups of customers. It is likely that, in most instances, key individual customers would be evaluated independently.

20.3.1   Generic evaluation of customer satisfaction

To enable the organisation to monitor this, it needs to define its means of measurement and how its is reported.

20.3.1.1   Measurement methods

The following grid, which takes the form of a tick list, may be used to define measurement methods. To ensure that no activity gets left out, all activities for which an 'Improvement action' form is generated in section 2 should automatically be added to the list.

	Development/evaluation method				
Action/company objective (e.g. from Improvement Action form)	Customer surveys	Customer visits	Balanced scorecard	Complaints record	Other
On-time delivery					
After-sales follow-up					
Invoicing accuracy					
Contact with key account manager	*Yes*	*Yes*	*No*	*Yes*	
Product returns reduction					
Executive contact with customers	*Yes*	*Yes*	*No*	*No*	
Other					
Other					

Note:
The development/evaluation methods and company objectives in the above grid are presented as an example only and do not reflect the wide range of options that are available or are being used by organisations. For each organisation, the final constitution of the grid will depend on its individual circumstances.

20.3.1.2   Reporting and communication

The results measured need to be communicated systematically to the right people within the organisation. To enable this, the following need to be addressed:

- Who/which department would results be provided to? (e.g. production, accounts, directors)

Executive sponsor, the executive board, sales and marketing teams, other groups as deemed appropriate

- What level of detail would be presented to each group?

Summary for directors, detailed briefing and reports to sales and marketing teams, etc.

- Who will take responsibility for producing and delivering the results?

Marketing manager

- How regularly would results be presented?

Monthly with a quarterly strategic review

- Who will collect, collate and analyse corrective/improvement suggestions from these groups?

Project leader, departmental managers

- Who will be responsible for carrying out improvement actions?

To be delegated as appropriate

20.4   Overview

The answers provided above are specifically for illustrative purposes only; they give an indication of how most of the tools provided in this book can be used to identify key areas for improvement, analyse, implement, review and communicate the relevant improvement activities.

REFERENCES

Adebanjo D. Understanding customer satisfaction - a UK food industry case study. *British Food Journal,* 2001, 103 (1), 36-45.

Anderson J.C., Narus J. Business Marketing: Understanding what customers value. *Harvard Business Review,* 1998, 53-65.

Anderson D. The secret behind that Wal-Mart smile. *Customer Management,* 2000, 12-13.

Anderson A. *Customer Satisfaction at Kraft Jacobs Suchard.* Internal presentation at the Customer Satisfaction Workgroup, 2000, Leatherhead Food RA, Leatherhead, UK.

Anon. *Coke recall is put at $60m.* Financial Times, 26 June 1999, London.

Anon. *Coca-Cola names sulphur as contaminant.* Financial Times, 19 June 1999, London.

Anon. *Coca-Cola hit by drinks scare in Europe.* Financial Times, 16 June 1999, London.

Anon. *You are the company.* www.fastcompany.com.

Anon. Does your customer service Rock'N'Roll. *Customer Management,* 2000, 6-11.

Anon. Handling complaints? You could do better! *Customer Management,* 2000, 35.

Anton J. Are you routed for success? *Customer Management,* 2000, 54-6.

Armistead C., Beamish N., Kiely J. *Emerging Skills for a Changing Economy.* Institute of Customer Service, 2001, UK.

Aschner G.S. Meeting customers' requirements and what can be expected. *The TQM Magazine,* 1999, 11 (6), 450-5.

Avlonas N. Exercising the loyalty prerogative. *Measuring Business Excellence,* 2000, 4 (1), 34-8.

Barlow N.M. Does your service have 'batteries included'? *Customer Management,* 2000, 48-51.

Bennett S. Hos jungle.com made up for primitive error. *Customer Management,* 2000, 8-10.

REFERENCES

Bhote K.R. *The Customer Loyalty Audit*. Pearson Education, London, 2000.

Bluestein A.I., Moriarty M., Sanderson R.J. *The Customer Satisfaction Audit*. Pearson Education, 2000.

Bowden P. A practical path to customer loyalty. *Qualityworld, 1998*.

Bowden P. Nortel's path to customer loyalty. *Measuring Business Excellence,* 1998, 2 (1), 8-13.

Charlesworth K., Ferguson N., Macdonald A., Mann S. UK plc needs to learn value of speaking customers' language. *Professional Manager,* 1999, 8 (5), 20-21.

Chase R.B., Aquilano N.J., Jacobs F.R. *Operations Management for Competitive Advantage*. McGraw-Hill, Irwin., 2001.

Christensen C.M., Tedlow R.S. Patterns of disruption in retailing. *Harvard Business Review,* 2000, 42-5.

Clague B. *Customer Satisfaction Case Study: TNT*. Internal presentation at the Customer Satisfaction Workgroup, 2000, Leatherhead Food RA, Leatherhead, UK.

Cohen L. *Quality Function Deployment*. Addison Wesley, Massachusetts., 1995.

Companies House. *Customer Satisfaction Survey*. The Register, Issue No. 44. (The magazine for Companies House customers), 2000.

Companies House. *What you can expect from companies house*. Customer report 5/99.

Contact organisation - Institute of Grocery Distribution (IGD). www.IGD.co.uk.

Cook S. *Customer Care*. Kogan Page, London, 2000.

Curry J. Lessons from the Pyramids. *Measuring Business Excellence,* 1997, 1 (1), 51-4.

Dennis B. Capturing customer perceptions. *Benchmark*. Periodic publication by the Civil Service College, UK, 1999.

Dick A.S., Basu K. Customer loyalty: toward an integrated conceptual framework. *Journal of the Academy of Marketing Science,* 1998, 22 (2), 99-113.

Downton S. e-Business in service. *Control,* 2000, 18-20.

Dunne D., Narasimhan C. The new appeal of private labels. *Harvard Business Review,* 1999, 41-52.

Eisenhardt K.M., Brown S.L. Time pacing: competing in markets that won't stand still. *Harvard Business Review,* 1998, 59-69.

EFQM model. www.efqm.org.

Erwin J. The six sigma focus on total customer satisfaction. *Measuring Business Excellence,* 1999, 2 (4), 16-22.

Federal Benchmarking Consortium *Serving the American Public: Best Practices in Resolving Customer Complaints.* National Performance Review commissioned by the Vice President of the United States, 1996.

Fisher M. What is the right supply chain for your product. *Harvard Business Review,* 1997, 105-116.

Galbreath J., Rogers T. Customer relationship leadership: a leadership and motivational model for the twenty-first century business. *The TQM Magazine,* 1999, 11 (3), 161-71.

Garcia P. Customer first or company last. *Customer Management,* 2000, 10-11.

Gardner R., Quigley S., Stone M. Nice data, shame about it's dissection. *Customer Management,* 2000, 30- 3.

Gilmore J.H., Pine J.B. II. The four faces of mass customization. *Harvard Business Review,* 1997, 75 (1), 91-101.

Gimein M. Sam Walton made a promise to us. *Fortune (Europe Edition),* 2002, 145 (6), 66-72.

Gober M. Increasing your confidence with complaints. *Customer Management,* 2000, 28-9.

Gowans S. Playing the loyalty card. *UK Excellence.* British Quality Foundation, 2001, 14-15.

Griffin J. *Customer Loyalty.* Jossey-Bass, San Francisco, 1997.

Gulati R., Garino J. Get the right mix of bricks and clicks. *Harvard Business Review,* 2000, 107-114.

Hill N. Customer satisfaction measurement. *Customer Service Management,* 1999, 39-42.

Hill N. Boost your response rates. *Customer Service Management,* 1999, 50-2.

Hill N. The seven stages of finding out what matters most to customers. *Measuring Business Excellence,* 1999, 3 (1), 31-5.

Hoffman D.L., Novak T.P. How to acquire customers on the web. *Harvard Business Review,* 2000, 78 (3), 179-88.

Holmstrom J., Hameri A. The dynamics of customer response. *International Journal of Operations and Production Management,* 1999, 19 (10), 993-1009.

Hutchins D. Managing a product recall. *Quality World,* 30-2.

REFERENCES

Industrial Society. *Customer Care.* Managing Best Practice Series, Industrial Society, London, 1995.

Johnston R. *Service Excellence = Reputation = Profit.* Institute of Customer Service, UK, 2001.

Kaplan R.S., Norton D.P. *The Balanced Scorecard.* Harvard Business School Press, Massachusetts, 1996.

Kemp J. What can you do to keep your customers loyal. *UK Excellence.* British Quality Foundation, 18, 2001.

Konijnendijk P.A. Dependence and conflict between production and sales. *Industrial Marketing Management,* 1993, 22, 161-7.

Kritchanchai D., MacCarthy B.L. Responsiveness of the order fulfilment process. *International Journal of Operations and Production Management,* 1999, 19 (8), 812-33.

Lampel J., Mintzberg H. Customising customisation. *Sloan Management Review,* 1996, 21-30.

Leingang J. Even the best can be better. *2000, Customer Management,* 6-9.

Lundahl L. ABB's EVITA puts customer-focused control centre stage. *Measuring Business Excellence,* 1997, 1 (3), 25-9.

Luxon M. Branding the facts. *UK Excellence.* British Quality Foundation, 2001, 16-17.

Mader R., Semenchuk J. From production to connection. *Measuring Business Excellence,* 2000, 4 (1), 46- 51.

Marra T. Put excellence into your CRM. *UK Excellence.* British Quality Foundation, 2001, 10-12.

Masella C., Rangone A. A contingent approach to the design of vendor selection systems for different types of co-operative customer/supplier relationships. *International Journal of Operations and Production Management,* 2000, 20 (1), 70-84.

McKinsey & Co. and CAPS Research. Coming into focus - using the lens of economic value to clarify the impact of B2B e-marketplaces. www.mckinsey.com or www.capsresearch.org. 2000.

McKinsey & Co. and CAPS Research. Coming into focus - using the lens of economic value to clarify the impact of B2B e-marketplaces. www.mckinsey.com or www.capsresearch.org. 2000.

Nunes P., Wilson D., Kambil A. The All-in-One Market. *Harvard Business Review,* 2000, 78 (3), 19-20.

Ormerod P. The ant and the consumer. *Measuring Business Excellence,* 1998, 2 (4), 38-43.

Parasuraman A., Zeithami V., Berry L.L. *Servqual: A multiple-Item Scale for Measuring Customer Perceptions of Service Quality,* Marketing Science Institute, 1986.

Patrick S. *Customer Satisfaction Measurement.* Internal presentation at the Customer Satisfaction Workgroup, 2000, Leatherhead Food RA, Leatherhead, UK.

Peppard J. Customer relationship management (CRM) in financial services. *European Management Journal,* 2000, 18 (3), 312-27.

Peters J. Beyond customer satisfaction. *Quality Focus,* 1999, 2 (6), 1.

Prahalad C.K., Ramaswamy V. Co-opting customer competence. *Harvard Business Review,* 2000, 79-87.

Reichheld F.F. Learning from customer defections. *Harvard Business Review,* 1996, 56-69.

Reichheld F.F., Schefter P. E-Loyalty: Your secret weapon on the web. *Harvard Business Review,* 2000, 78 (4), 105-13.

Rigby D.K., Reichheld F.F., Schefter P. Avoiding the four perils of CRM. *Harvard Business Review,* 2002, 101-109.

Romeijn A. How to produce better service. *Measuring Business Excellence,* 1999, 3 (2), 16-21.

Routledge C. Take no prisoners with customer loyalty. *UK Excellence.* British Quality Foundation, 2001, 6-8.

Seybold P.B. Get inside the lives of your customers. *Harvard Business Review,* 2001, 81-9.

Sinha I. Cost transparency: The net's real threat to prices and brands. *Harvard Business Review,* 2000, 43- 50.

Slywotzky A.J. Patterns of disruption in retailing. *Harvard Business Review,* 2000, 40-1.

Smith I. *Meeting Customer Needs.* Butterworth Heinemann, Oxford, 1997.

Sörqvist L. At the cutting edge of data gathering. *Measuring Business Excellence,* 1999, 3 (4), 36-41.

Spring M., Dalrymple J.F. Product customisation and manufacturing strategy. *International Journal of Operations and Production Management,* 2000, 20 (4), 441-67.

Stone C.L., Banks M.J. The use of customer- and employee-based performance measures, in The Times Top 500 Companies. *The TQM Magazine,* 1997, 9 (2), 152-8.

Stone M. Customer careless. *Customer Management,* 2000, 42-7.

Stone M., Woodcock N., Machtynger L. *Customer Relationship Marketing*, Kogan Page, London, 1997.

Strand T. Heroes and villains. *Customer Management*, 2000, 15.

Sturley S. *Customers want food solutions - so how do Brakes tackle that?* Presentation at the Customer Service Network, 2001.

TMI & ICS. *National Complaints Culture Survey 2001*. TMI, UK (www.tmi.co.uk). 2001.

TMI & ICS. *National Complaints Culture Survey 2001*. TMI, UK (www.tmi.co.uk). 2001.

Wakeling B. Rapid response vehicle. *Measuring Business Excellence*, 1998, 2 (1), 14-17.

Whiteley R., Hessan D. Customer-centred growth: Five strategies for building competitive advantage. *Quality Focus*, 1999, 2 (6), 2-7.

Wilcox T. Helping customers to help themselves. *Customer Management*, 2000, 44-5.

Customer Service Organisations and Other Sources of Information

1. The Institute of Customer Service
   2 Castle Court
   St Peter's Street
   Colchester   www.ics-nto.com
   Essex   enquiries@instcustserv.com
   CO1 1EW   Tel: 01206 571716
   UK

2. Customer Service Network
   Berrington Lodge   www.customernet.com
   91-93 Tettenhall Road www.learningfromeachother.com
   Wolverhampton   Tel: 01902 311641
   WV3 9NQ

3. British Quality Foundation
   32-34 Great Peter Street   www.quality-foundation.co.uk
   London   Tel: 0207 654 5000
   SW1P 2QX

4. The University of Liverpool Management School
   The University of Liverpool
   Liverpool   www.liverpool.ac.uk
   L69 3GH
   UK

5. Customer 1st International
   Bramblewood House   Tel: 01985 841070
   Frog Lane   e-mail: stephanie@customer1st.uk.com
   Longbridge Deverill
   Wiltshire
   BA12 7DS
   UK

6. Warwick Business School
   The University of Warwick   www.wbs.warwick.ac.uk
   Coventry
   CV4 7AL
   UK

7. Unisys Management Today Service Excellence Awards
   Unisys Ltd
   Tongwell Street   www.serviceexcellenceawards.com
   Fox Milne   www.clicktools.com
   Milton Keynes
   MK15 0YS
   UK

Case Study Organisations

1. Pernod Ricard
2. British Telecommunications plc
3. Magro Brothers (Foods) Ltd
4. Northern Ireland Electricity (part of Viridian plc)
5. Kraft Foods UK Ltd
6. Customer Satisfaction Workgroup of the Benchmarking Club for the Food and Drinks Industry.

Acknowledgements

This book was made possible through the efforts and contributions of numerous people in industry. Their experiences have led to an improved understanding of customer satisfaction leverage and change factors. Particular mention goes to the following: Steve Keen, John Magro, Fred Mahoney, Graham Wills, Ann Anderson, David Smith, Daniel McLarnon, Nicola Patel, Colin Milsom, Rebecca Williams and members of the Benchmarking Club.

The resources required for the research and production of the book were provided by DEFRA (formerly MAFF). My sincere gratitude goes to them. A special thank you goes to Dr Christina Goodacre for her support over the years.

For their careful review of the manuscript and their constructive comments: Steve Keen (again), Stephanie Edwards, Simon Snowden, Mark Bradley and Professor Dennis Kehoe.

My appreciation goes to the Leatherhead crew, Vivienne Pride, Ann Pernet, Sharon Coe, Paul Homewood and Victoria Emerton for their hard work on the manuscript. Finally, I would like to thank members of the Benchmarking Institute for their support and contributions to the literature review.

Dr Dotun Adebanjo